Inspiring | Educating | Creating | Entertaining

Brimming with creative inspiration, how-to projects, and useful information to enrich your everyday life, quarto.com is a favorite destination for those pursuing their interests and passions.

First Published in 2023 by Cool Springs Press, an imprint of The Quarto Group,
100 Cummings Center, Suite 265-D,
Beverly, MA 01915, USA.
T (978) 282-9590 F (978) 283-2742 Quarto.com

Cool Springs Press titles are also available at discount for retail, wholesale, promotional, and bulk purchase. For details, contact the Special Sales Manager by email at specialsales@quarto.com or by mail at The Quarto Group, Attn: Special Sales Manager, 100 Cummings Center, Suite 265-D, Beverly, MA 01915, USA.

27 26 25 24 23   1 2 3 4 5

ISBN: 978-0-7603-7623-2

Digital edition published in 2023
eISBN: 978-0-7603-7624-9

Library of Congress Cataloging-in-Publication Data

Names: Gardner, Graham Laird, author.
Title: Tiny + wild : build a small-scale meadow anywhere / Graham Laird Gardner.
Other titles: Tiny and wild
Description: Beverly, MA : Cool Springs Press, 2023. | Includes index. | Summary: "Tiny & Wild is the essential guide to creating a small-scale mini meadow that's filled with low-maintenance plants to please both pollinators and people"— Provided by publisher.
Identifiers: LCCN 2022045241 (print) | LCCN 2022045242 (ebook) | ISBN 9780760376232 (trade paperback) | ISBN 9780760376249 (ebook)
Subjects: LCSH: Meadows. | Meadow gardening. | Meadow plants. | Meadow ecology.
Classification: LCC SB439 .G297 2023 (print) | LCC SB439 (ebook) | DDC 578.74/6--dc23/eng/20220928
LC record available at https://lccn.loc.gov/2022045241
LC ebook record available at https://lccn.loc.gov/2022045242

Design and page layout: Laura Shaw Design
Cover Images: Graham Laird Gardner (front, top left and top middle), Adam Woodruff (front, top right), Ali Hussain (front, bottom), JLY Gardens (back)

All photos by Graham Laird Gardener except:
Rob Cardillo Photography and Phyto Studios: p. 23
JLY Gardens: pp. 10, 11, 30, 31, 32, 35, 37, 39, 40, 41T, 51T, 51BL, 52, 59, 62, 63, 69, 71, 73TR, 79TR, 84, 85, 86, 89T, 93, 98TL, 100T, 104TR, 108L, 109, 111L, 114, 115, 119, 127TL, 134TL, 157TR, 160TR
Holly Shields: pp. 41B, 102TL
Hayden Regina: pp. 26TL, 26TR, 27, 136
Shutterstock: pp. 16, 34TL, 34TR, 36TR, 38, 43T, 54, 55, 70, 88, 90, 104TL, 105, 106TL, 123TL, 127 TR, 134TR
Benjamin Vogt: pp. 13, 56L, 89B
Scott Weber: pp. 28L, 28R, 29
Claudia West: p. 172
Adam Woodwruff: pp. 6, 24, 25T, 25B, 36TL, 116, 139, 161TL
Kevin Philip Williams: p. 8BL

Printed in China

Tiny + Wild

Build a Small-Scale Meadow Anywhere

GRAHAM LAIRD GARDNER

COOL
SPRINGS
PRESS

Contents

OPPOSITE Welcoming spontaneity by thoughtful design, a dense flower-
forward meadow can thrive in the most challenging spaces.

Why a Mini Meadow?

The Benefits of Growing a Small-Scale Meadow

Welcome. You've heard the calling—for a more resilient biodiverse garden, full of flowers and movement, that is inspired by natural plant communities and the wild spaces around you. Perhaps you feel a sense of nostalgia for the wilderness of your childhood or a need to invite wild places home.

Do you have a balcony or an underperforming section of yard? Maybe you have an area of lawn you wish to convert, or a section of your veggie plot you'd like to devote to attracting more pollinators and other beneficial insects? However, you are not quite sure where to begin.

You've taken hikes, visited gardens, snapped photos, gathered ideas, and are now looking to create your own tiny meadow. This book is for you. Whether you are an avid gardener, or a total novice, we will delve into how to site, design, prepare, plant, and maintain a meadow that suits your space, aesthetic, and local growing conditions.

In this book, you'll learn why naturalistic planting design is important and explore how to channel inspiration from wild and designed spaces into a customized version for yourself. We will discuss how to evaluate your property and select the best site for your project. I'll help you to understand basic principles of successful design and help to clarify a process that is right for you. We will go over how to prepare the area, as well as how to best lay out and install your plants.

A pair of goldfinches pause on a coneflower amongst salvia, sea holly, and allium.

Purple prairie clover (*Dalea purpurea*), Aspen fleabane (*Erigeron speciosus*), narrow-leaf coneflower (*Echinacea angustifolia*), and yellow coneflower (*Echinacea paradoxa*).

Meadow maintenance is included, along with how this maintenance will change—becoming easier over time as your mini meadow becomes more established. We will also view sample plant lists with species suggestions for different applications and climates.

Design Inspired By Nature

Design inspired by nature has been my preference for as far back as I can remember. My grandparents introduced me to a love of the wild and gardening at a young age. That passion and reverence has never left. Have you ever arrived at the crest of a hill and discovered a field of vibrant wildflowers awaiting you on the other side? Have you entered a clearing in the forest filled with blooming forbs and grasses backlit in contrast to your shaded stroll? Do you recall the sense of joy and awe these moments of discovery provided? This book will help you capture that essence and transport it to your home.

The Essence of a Meadow at Any Scale

Many people think of meadows as large open wild spaces or acres of agricultural land. Here we will distill those vast landscapes into plant collections that fit your site. Squint your eyes and transpose that texture, energy, and seasonality into a container, corner, or entire lot. Inspired, you may decide to fill a few containers with a dozen plants or create a new garden bed with many more. The sum of these small efforts is greater than their individual moments of beauty. Together, they offer a patchwork of habitat, forage, and cover—pathways for pollinators, food for songbirds, and delight for humans.

The beauty of a butterfly floating from umbel to umbel, a hummingbird hovering in front of a cardinal flower, or a goldfinch dangling from a seed head is something in which everyone can find joy. Our busy weeks and hectic lifestyles deserve these moments of pause in our daily lives. It's incredible to go on hikes and explore wild places in distant preserves. We can invite that into our own properties with simple research and planning so nature can be enjoyed each time we pass through the yard or gaze out the window.

TOP, LEFT Find inspiration in wild places like this one. Purple elephant's head (*Pedicularis groenlandica*) weaves through a wet meadow beside a mountain lake.

BOTTOM, LEFT Awash in color and abundant in species diversity, this meadow provides numerous options to stimulate your imagination.

OPPOSITE The layers of this densely planted mini meadow are tucked into a narrow site along a fence line in a parking lot.

Are All Flower Gardens Meadows?

The short answer is no. Meadow-esque gardens are densely planted with a strong element of grasses or grass-like species interweaving the plantings. The challenge is to emulate natural plant communities in the layers, patterns, and spontaneity. Traditional perennial plantings may have more rigid spacing with gaps in between each plant—neatly laid out in clean discernable grids or some symmetrical patterns. Conventional gardens may also emphasize the flower displays versus how the plants interact and how the design reads overall. Meadow gardens have more whimsy. This requires forethought in design to capture, but is ultimately more forgiving in the long run. Naturalistic planting also tends to reflect elements of the regions in which they are created. While traditional designs often reuse the same species all over the world, meadow designs set themselves apart by offering an opportunity to celebrate local species and regional aesthetics.

Naturalistic garden design that emulates or references native plant communities is more than just beautiful. One of the major advantages over traditional perennial garden design is that it can be maintained as a system. Instead of managing each plant independently, you can approach the care of the garden as a unit. Over time, as the planting layers weave together and become more established, maintenance is greatly reduced. Depending on how involved you wish to be, maintenance can be as simple as an annual cut back, periodic weeding, and perhaps an occasional supplemental watering during extended periods of drought to keep your mini meadow looking it's best.

This traditional perennial border needs more species-specific maintenance than a meadow garden by including species such as daylilies that require labor intensive deadheading to look their best.

Lawns + Alternatives

For high traffic areas and sports fields, turfgrass has its place. Outside of those applications, however, it has become an overused landscape default. Often, property owners will eliminate existing vegetation with little discernment for what's there in favor of a neatly clipped turfgrass. Familiarity with this choice and its accompanying maintenance, as well as influence from abutting properties, has created a go-to choice that is in need of reevaluation. One theory is that humans prefer low vegetation due to an innate primal fear of large predators and a desire to feel safe. Why mow: that is the question.

Historically, land was used for cultivating crops and as grazing areas for livestock. Having an area devoted to lawn and not food production indicated wealth. This has trickled down as an indicator of socio-economic status and been copied with little consideration as to the reason why. Turf is now the largest single irrigated crop in the United States, covering over forty million acres of land.

If all of that acreage was watered at the recommended amount of one inch (2.5 cm) per week, it's estimated that would require two-hundred gallons (909 L) of fresh water per person per day. In addition to requiring vast amounts of water, turf maintenance has a large carbon footprint. Did you know that one hour of lawn mowing generates the same pollution as driving three hundred miles (483 km) in a car? Add to that the fertilizers and pesticides required to achieve the perfect lawn texture and color. You may wish to rethink the proportion of your property that is covered in turf.

By starting with a small meadow, you will learn how to create something that can be expanded upon in the future. By converting more of your high maintenance and high input lawn into a low maintenance meadow, you will be creating a high value habitat for pollinators and other wildlife. As with cooking, once you experiment with the proper preparation and ingredients you can double the recipe.

One hour of lawn mowing generates the same pollution as driving three hundred miles (483 km) in a car. Time to rethink the amount of your property devoted to lawn.

LEFT This low-water, low-maintenance garden is filled with plants selected to thrive in dry, sunny conditions.

OPPOSITE Even dressed all in green, this front yard shines amongst its neighbors and is filled with texture and movement.

Resiliency + Biodiversity: A Paradigm Shift

The interest in, and preference for, naturalistic planting design is part of a greater movement toward ecological landscape management. There is more awareness now of how our individual choices impact the climate. Learning about biodiversity loss and species extinction can feel overwhelming. This book centers on hope and personal empowerment. Regardless of the size of your property, you get to make choices that will affect your local environment. As you become more informed about an ecological approach to landscaping and why it's important, you will have the opportunity to share this knowledge—inspiring friends and neighbors to think differently. As each of your connections create their own mini meadows, a patchwork of more biodiverse habitat will result.

Whatever your reason for selecting this book, you now have it in your hands. Read it with a pen to mark useful passages. Write in the margins. Keep a journal nearby to jot down ideas as you read. While I have written it in the order in which I would approach a new project, you needn't read it cover to cover before you begin preparing your site or designing your garden. Familiarize yourself with the chapters and their contents. You may wish to read as you go, dividing your project into phases that correlate with the sequence of the book. By chapter three you will have a good foundation as to how to select a site and begin designing. We will begin by highlighting places to find inspiration—both in wild and man-made spaces.

Finding Wild Inspiration in Natural + Man-Made Spaces

Using Natural Plant Communities and Existing Public Gardens to Spark Your Creativity

A Sense of Place

We've heard the phrase "a sense of place," but what does it mean to you? Perhaps it's my background, but for me, this often starts with the local plant palette. When I go for a walk in a wild or semi-wild space, what flowers do I observe? What do the plant communities look like? What colors are the rocks and soil? Are there mountains, forests, prairies, or palm trees? What are the predominant shades of the leaves? Is it a lush or sparse landscape? Locale is a critical element in design. It's what makes a place unique and in turn informs the built environment.

When you're looking through travel photos on Instagram or in blogs, what sets each place apart? I think of the architecture—the choices of materials and paints as well as the designs and history. Then there is the clothing, fashion, fabrics, and colors. Maybe you think of the cuisine and its ingredients and preparations. These are just a few examples of what makes a place distinct. Notice these elements are also influenced by local climates and ecosystems. What excites you to visit a new place? When seeking inspiration for a garden, especially a meadow, I encourage you to find the clues locally.

Observe + Be Inspired

Landscape design inspiration comes from many places including garden visits, books, photography,

Flowers and seedheads punctuate this grassy street planting on a challenging site.

Take time to study and identify the species that pique your curiosity. There is so much information in the wild spaces around you that will guide you toward success.

Bring a camera, hand lens, notebook, and plant ID book or app on your nature walks.

travel, and nature. The wild places around you offer glimpses of landscapes that are thriving without maintenance and inputs. Tolerant of local conditions, the plant communities and their individual species are an informative place to start when looking for ideas. Look at how the assemblages (collections of plants) change based on typography, proximity to water, elevation, and other factors that influence microclimates.

See how these characteristics differ based on where you travel. Perhaps there are subtle shifts between the coastline and nearby forests or more distinct differences between the eastern and western slopes of a local mountain range. It's possible to be inspired by different environments nearby and then consider how you might combine them in a novel way. Always start with exploring places close to your project site and expand out from there.

Learn to ID: Wildflower Guides + Keys

When you go on your morning jog or a weekend hike with your family, pay attention to the plants around you. What do you find beautiful? Purchase a native plant guide for your area. Learn how to identify what you are seeing. I suggest beginners find a book arranged by flower color.

You may also wish to experiment with a wildflower book that has a botanical key. Botanical keys are actually quite easy and useful once you get the hang of it. Most methods involve observation of three plant parts: the flower, the plant type and branching pattern, and the leaf. Admittedly, getting started can be intimidating, but they are one of the best ways to ensure a quick and accurate identification. Fortunately, there are also a few plant identification apps available that can be as simple as uploading a picture or answering a few questions. Find the best one for your area. Once you have a couple of tools to help you with identifying what you are observing, start a list of your favorite plants.

OPPOSITE Use the colors of the rocks, soils, and plant communities near you to inspire a planting unique to your area.

Making Friends with Local Experts: Join a Native Plant Society

Find a native plant society in your area and check out their website. Perhaps they have online plant lists and book recommendations. Maybe they have links to articles and other resources. One of my favorite ways to learn is to attend walks with local guides. This offers you the chance to learn and meet new friends with varying degrees of expertise. You will be able to ask questions in the field in a relaxed setting with other curious enthusiasts like yourself. Much knowledge can be obtained and exchanged in such gatherings. Once you've begun to make a list of species that interest you, ask the group about their experiences with them. This may be an opportunity for you to begin a master list (or spreadsheet) where you'll collect data based on your research. See chapters three and seven for more information on how to do this.

Observing and Attracting Local Creatures

Another aspect to consider is the wildlife you'd like to attract. What birds, bees, and butterflies have you observed nearby? Consider keeping a list of these as well. When researching plants for your new meadow, you may be able to include larval host plants for the caterpillars of the butterflies you wish to attract—or plants that offer habitat or nesting material to certain bird species. Gardens based on the local ecology offer a fascinating opportunity to foster plant-wildlife interactions.

While some insects are generalists, meaning they will be happy foraging, nesting, and reproducing amongst different plant species, many insects are specialists that require specific species with which they've evolved. Take the monarch for example. It lays its eggs on milkweed (*Asclepias*) species. If you live in North America and are within the flyways of the monarchs' migration, you have extra incentive to include *Asclepias* species that work with your site conditions.

A simple way to support local pollinators is to provide nectar and pollen sources throughout the growing season—from early spring to late fall. See chapter seven for suggested species and their bloom times. This allows you to attract a diversity of pollinators. You may then wish to record these visitors and do further research on those that you identify. Learning the local insects and other wildlife takes time and observation, but a meadow garden of any size is an excellent way to start.

Join a native plant group to meet experts and novices alike and learn about the plant communities and landscapes around you in an informal setting.

Many insects are specialists that require specific species, like this Monarch caterpillar on a butterfly milkweed (*Asclepias tuberosa*), with which they've evolved.

With an elongated body perfect for climbing inside these spotted beebalm (*Monarda punctata*) flowers, this elegant black wasp was observed visiting only these species in this planting.

Planting for Wildlife

Do you delight in seeing a butterfly or dragonfly? Do you love to close your eyes and listen to the birds? Do the sounds of toads peeping in spring as they wake from their winter slumber offer you hope of green to come? Are you alarmed by the loss of bees and other insects, and feel the calling to support them? Celebrating wildlife isn't just reserved for David Attenborough specials. It's happening right outside your window and your conscious connection to it begins with curiosity.

Do you remember turning over a log in the forest to check for salamanders and centipedes? Or cradling a baby blue egg in your hands to show your mother? Did you have a net and a magnifying glass as a child? Do you keep your birdfeeder full of seeds? Are you like me with countless videos on your phone featuring closeups of pollinators?

If you build it, they will come. Planting for wildlife can be as focused or as general as you make it. It can be the primary reason for your new meadow or an added bonus. As will discuss in the goals section in chapter 2, take time to consider if there is anything specific you hope to attract. Practice observation. What do you see in the wild and man-made areas around your home? Research those animals and insects that pique your interest. Get a field guide for your area. Find out the plant and floral associations that would give you better odds of a visit.

Traditional chemically treated lawns are relatively devoid of ecology. Once you begin introducing meadow and prairie plants, you automatically increase the biodiversity on your property, no matter how small. Suddenly you invite more life to share your space with you. Your tiny meadow, when considered with those of neighbors and friends, creates a patchwork or mosaic of habitat that connects urban green spaces to wild preserves. Wildlife gardens can be any size! This network supports the safe movement of wildlife between larger natural areas.

Butterflies + Bees + Birds

A great spangled fritillary butterfly floats from umbel to umbel in drifts of statuesque Joe-Pye weeds in a late summer meadow.

This sculptural pollinator hotel provides shelter and nesting sites for a variety of local pollinators using simple materials found nearby.

A skipper butterfly extends its proboscis to sip the nectar of this New York ironweed (*Vernonia noveboracensis*).

This orb weaver invites us to unlearn our misplaced fear of spiders, observe the beauty of their intricate webs, and study their vital function in the landscape.

BEES

FOOD Provide a diversity of flower shapes and colors (with a large proportion of plants native to your area) that bloom, ideally consecutively/continuously, over a long period of time; stick to straight species and avoid popular hybridized varieties that may have had their nectar/pollen reduced by their breeding and selection; offer a water source such as a shallow birdbath with stones or a pile of sand/gravel so it can be accessed without drowning.

SHELTER/HABITAT Leave bare patches of soil for ground-nesting bees; leave your plant stems up for the winter and try to find a place on site to stack them when you cut them back; consider building a bee house or hotel—just be sure to do your research and keep it cleaned as instructed; if you have the space, leave a dead tree or stump standing.

FUN FACT One out of every three bites of our food depends on pollinators. There are twenty thousand species of bees around the world, and most are solitary.

BUTTERFLIES

FOOD Grow locally native plants and plants with nectar flowers; identify the species of butterflies in your area and select their larval host plants (many butterfly caterpillars only dine on certain species)—such as milkweed for monarchs and parsley or dill for swallowtails; place a shallow tray of water nearby as described in the bee section; consider sharing your overripe fruit for an occasional treat (just be sure to move it to the compost in the evening to avoid attracting any undesirable wildlife); leave open soil in a low area as an intermittent puddle—butterflies are often found gathering salts and minerals in the mud.

SHELTER/HABITAT Full sun, low wind locations are favored by butterflies; plan for all of the life stages including eggs/larvae/caterpillars/chrysalides; include grasses and possibly an artfully positioned pile of local rocks for shelter from rains; consider creating a brush pile and allow for leaf litter to remain year-round in strategic locations; grasses and other upright stems provide safe locations for chrysalis to form.

FUN FACT Butterflies taste with their feet. These receptors help them find their host plants on which to lay their eggs.

BIRDS

FOOD Select seed-bearing and nectar-rich flowers; locally native plants attract native insects; attracting butterflies means more caterpillars for young birds; leave the leaf litter to increase the insect populations; add a birdbath or multiple birdbaths depending upon how many visitors you get; consider adding movement like a circulating pump that bubbles; add a heater in the winter; offer a variety of high-quality bird seed and suet cakes in the off season; nuts and fruit will also attract various species; plant red tubular flowers for hummingbirds and supplement with a nectar feeder of sugar water; site your feeders where you can enjoy them year-round and close to shrubs and other cover for safety; use baffles to discourage squirrels; clean feeders regularly.

SHELTER/HABITAT Be sure there is shelter and dense, layered cover nearby such as trees, shrubs, and herbaceous plantings (like your new mini meadow); find a place for a brush pile; place your Christmas tree outside near your birdfeeders once you've taken it down for the season; add bird houses suitable for any species you wish to attract; offer nesting materials like hair from your brush, fur from your pets, natural strings/yarn and place in suet cage; keep your cats indoors and place a bell on their collar in case they escape.

FUN FACT It takes six thousand to nine thousand caterpillars to raise one clutch (number of hatchings in one nesting period) of chickadees.

Reduce or eliminate pesticide use on your property

To attract and support wildlife, commit to reducing or eliminating all synthetic pesticides and fertilizers from your landscape. Opt for non-toxic or organic practices—or don't use any at all. If you must, start with the least toxic option and always follow the label. Not only will this protect the animals and insects, it will also protect and help build the life in your soil.

Think of your landscape holistically—a mini-ecosystem. Instead of running to grab a spray when you see aphids, wait and check for lady beetle, lacewing, or other beneficial insect eggs. It could be that by you spraying, even with an organic formulation, you are disrupting the natural cycle in your garden. Practice patience, by taking a step back and observing. Allow the diversity of your local ecosystem to grow.

Find an acceptable threshold of damage before you intervene. Even if the aphids or other pests disfigure a few plants, those plants will survive. If you don't interrupt by altruistic micromanagement, you may find that the beneficial insect population increases and keeps them in check in the future.

Scout, identify, research, monitor, and enjoy. Unlearn your fears and find the awe and fascination in these interactions. Learn to love the perfection in the imperfect—knowing you are supporting life with your choices. Take pictures and record what you see.

Additional Resources for Inspiration + Knowledge

This book is a primer for creating your mini meadow. My experience is based on years of experimentation, practice, and exposure to beautiful gardens, landscapes, images, and designers—and books about the processes. This includes my mistakes, which taught me valuable lessons and helped me grow as a designer. There is a resources section on page 168 with a list of some of my favorite gardens, designers, and books on this topic. If you have the time, in addition to exploring the wild spaces around you, familiarize yourself with some of these resources.

Learn more about meadow gardens, naturalistic planting design, and ecological landscaping. If you're on social media, follow planting designers, landscape architects, horticulturists, and botanic garden staff that work in this style. I've included a short list of suggested hashtags to follow in the resource section. Hashtags introduce us to designers and projects that may be up and coming or off the radar, as well as allow us to follow along with our favorites. In addition to the legendary designers, you'll find the work of other talented folks who share the vision and language of the movement.

Another important resource are your local nurseries. Visit and support them. Introduce yourself to the staff and ask questions. Peruse their inventory and plant catalogues. Ask them where to see examples of designed meadows and naturalistic landscapes nearby. If you're fortunate enough to live near public gardens or botanic gardens that celebrate naturalistic planting design, go explore them and be sure to see them at different times of year.

If you reach for a spray—even an organic one—you may disrupt the delicate ecosystem of your garden and accidentally kill the beneficial insects you hope to attract. Notice the lady beetle laying eggs that will soon eat these orange oleander aphids.

OPPOSITE Botanic gardens are filled with information and inspiration like this Pollinator Garden in the Arboretum at Penn State University.

Case Studies: Aspirational Designed Meadows

In addition to inspiration from wild places, it's important to have designed landscapes to reference. The following are a few of my favorite mini meadow gardens. On the coast, on the roof, and on the sidewalk—these gardens demonstrate what's possible. While the designers are celebrated professionals, their process includes the same basic steps that you will take. Let their knowledge and success embolden you and seek out other examples that speak to you.

REDSTONE LANE | Marblehead, Massachusetts, United States of America

DESIGNER Adam Woodruff

Adam Woodruff is well-traveled with an astute eye, deep plant knowledge, and a talented and savvy circle of planting design friends. His own backyard in Marblehead, Massachusetts, is both art and classroom—where he can play, observe, and continually improve.

The site is adjacent to a right-of-way and ship-yard. Creating privacy while maintaining views to the harbor is achieved by strategic grading and hedge placement. Being coastal means the plant palette is limited to those species that thrive in a seaside location. The design is considered using both the views while in the house as well as the experience of being in the garden. Plants are selected based on their bloom and duration, foliage textures, fragrance, and winter interest.

One of the tricks that Adam shares is the use of diagonals to organize the design. By committing to a readable pattern, the garden is easier to maintain and creates the illusion of more space. He intersperses taller emergent plants strategically to build in a feeling of spontaneity. By monitoring the species during establishment, he's able to encourage species based on how they perform in the space.

While the design evokes the spontaneity of a stylized meadow, each plant has been thoughtfully placed. Evaluating bloom succession and seasonal interest, Adam continues to refine his choices as he learns more about how the species he has selected interact with each other on his site. He fine-tunes the balance of the composition by thoughtful edits as the garden matures.

LEFT When carefully designed, the same small space can look like entirely different gardens throughout the seasons.

OPPOSITE, TOP Note the species diversity in the layers of this densely planted meadow.

OPPOSITE, BOTTOM Considering the shapes and textures of each species, plants are selected for seasonal interest both in and out of flower.

DESIGNER Hayden Regina

Notice how the same view of a small space changes throughout the seasons.

While reddish-pink echinacea pops in the photo on the left, drifts of deep orange yarrow punctuate the photo above.

TINY + WILD

Hayden Regina's Chicago, Illinois, rooftop is a colorful haven in the city for wildlife and humans alike. Were it not for the surrounding skyline, you might not know you were on a roof—nor would you guess that the garden is only entering its second growing season. The fifth story site is hot in summer and windy in the winter, so plants were selected accordingly.

Like the other designers featured in these case studies, Hayden was inspired by the work of Dutch designer Piet Oudolf, especially the nearby Lurie Garden at Millennium Park as well as the Midwest prairie landscapes where he grew up. His focus was on texture and flower shape more than color—though the planting is not lacking in

that regard. He employed a matrix style approach that uses intermixed repetition and limits large groupings of the same species. Selecting compact cultivars of larger prairie and meadow species allowed him to fit a multitude of diverse species in a small space. He also thoughtfully edits volunteer seedlings and plans to overseed with prairie grasses to encourage more diversity and spontaneity.

The design capitalizes on the city views and encourages a lingering pause as you pass through the planting moving between the dining and sitting areas. As the garden is on the roof, the planting medium is lightweight and shallow. To accommodate for these extreme conditions and

The purple foliage of these penstemon contrasts against the vibrant green of spring.

less soil temperature regulation, Hayden selected plants that were hardy to areas colder than his region. Before renovating, he used the first season to test species in pots for their durability. Most young plants were installed as landscape plugs and one-quart (1 L) pots. There is dripline snaked throughout to provide supplemental watering during heat spells and droughts. It's a learning landscape in which to experiment and observe that is simple to maintain with an annual late winter cut back.

DESIGNER Scott Weber

The gardens spill across the sidewalk, blurring the line between public and private spaces.

A densely planted bulb layer of white and purple allium shines in mid-spring.

Scott Weber's property in Portland, Oregon, is brimming with plants. When he ran out of space in his main yard, he decided to leap the sidewalk and take on the parking strip, sometimes referred to as a hell strip due to the challenging conditions. He removed the existing sod in February 2012. In contrast to the heavy clay found elsewhere in his landscape, he discovered light well-drained soil below.

He created a planting plan and continually reworked it as he dreamed of how the combinations of plants would work best together and discovered a new species he wanted to include. It's a garden with a foundation of urban-tolerant grasses with perennial flowers dotted throughout. As a high-use location with on-street parking, he created a setback from the road to allow for car doors to open and a path for visitors to pass through without trampling the plants.

Scott admits that the garden has changed quite a bit since the initial design and embraces the process that is inevitable for a dynamic planting with a passionate gardener. He used a combination of cuttings, divisions, and plants he grew from seed as well as some purchased specifically for this location. By propagating from plants he already had in his other gardens, he tied the new site back to the landscape around the house.

Scott writes the Rhone Street Gardens blog, where he shares his gardening experiences and travels with his followers. He takes cues from nature as well as noted designers in the New Perennial Movement and naturalistic plantings using the patterns and textures of wild plant communities as inspiration for his designs.

OPPOSITE, BOTH The same view at different times of year. When considering design, Dutch designer Piet Oudolf reminds us that "brown is also a color."

Assessing Landscapes

At this point, you've begun to tune into your surroundings in a new way — finding inspiration in the wild and designed spaces around you. You've assembled some resources to help you identify and record what you've observed. You may have even begun to see new connections between plants and wildlife that you hadn't noticed before. We've looked at three case studies to learn how these aspirational gardens have been created— including site considerations and aesthetic preference that helped to guide these experts in their design process. Hopefully you've begun to consider how these projects may inspire and inform your own.

In the next chapter we will explore how to look at your own landscape in new ways. You will learn how to assess various sites for your new garden—recording and analyzing the conditions and elements unique to your landscape. We'll look at examples of possible locations and examine limitations and opportunities that will help you get started finding the perfect spot for a mini meadow of your own.

LEFT The soft blue of woodland phlox (*Phlox divaricata*) weaves between the vibrant green textures of sedge (*Carex* sp.).

OPPOSITE The delicate reflexed flowers of this pale purple coneflower (*Echinacea pallida*) dance in the breeze above the foliage.

2

Bringing the Meadow Home

Site Selection Advice to Find the Ideal Spot for Planting and Learning How to Work with Existing Conditions

Having this book in your hands means you're invested in learning more about how to build a small-scale meadow of your own. You've discovered initial inspiration and are wondering how to capture that essence and invite it home to your property. Finding the ideal location means asking the right questions and doing a little exploring. We will review how to capture the key details you'll need as well as go through some possible locations. These examples will help you better understand what to consider as you explore your own landscape.

If this is new to you, that's okay! We will keep it simple and fun. One important piece of information that will guide you in your project is a list of goals. They will keep you focused. You will circle back to these throughout the process. We will

learn how to identify and evaluate them for your own project. You're on the path and will learn the steps to set yourself up for success. A beautiful flourishing meadow awaits!

Exploring Your Landscape with New Eyes: Inventory + Analysis

Let's begin by finding the perfect location for your new project. Creating a new garden starts by evaluating possible sites. Even if you have lived in your home for many years, taking on a new garden project will benefit from a fresh perspective. To better familiarize yourself with your property, one of the first steps is to do an inventory and analysis. To do this, take an inventory of

This mini meadow is rich in diversity, combining pale purple coneflower (*Echinacea pallida*), Carthusian pink (*Dianthus carthusianorum*), 'Hummelo' betony (*Betonica officinalis* 'Hummelo'), cultivated knotweed (*Koenigia polystachya*), Mexican feathergrass (*Nassella tenuissima*), and more, with the broad blue-green leaves and towering flower stems of the large coneflower (*Rudbeckia maxima*) set to bloom in the foreground.

This young landscape would benefit from a mini meadow planted in and around the gravel of the drainage swale by selecting species best suited for those conditions.

Imagine interrupting this large expanse of turf with a flower meadow, creating separate rooms between the covered patio, swing set, and play lawn.

the existing elements and site conditions in your landscape. Existing elements include items such as walkways, outbuildings, retaining walls, fences, existing plants, and other site features. Site conditions include the sun and shade exposure, moist and dry areas, and the soil type and pH. Once you have taken a closer look at these items, you will then interpret and analyze them to better understand any limitations and opportunities for improvement. Not to worry, we will be reviewing the basics of these steps over the next few pages, so you'll see how simple yet important these observations are. Both inventory and analysis give you clues and puzzle pieces to create an informed design. As a landscape designer, I encourage my clients to consider their entire property when first beginning a project. If you already have an idea and location in mind, you may wish to focus your attention on this spot. The practice of reading the landscape, taking notes, and interpreting them will help you locate and evaluate a perfect location to install your new planting.

OPPOSITE Hoary vervain (*Verbena stricta*) and purple coneflower (*Echinacea purpurea*) make a vibrant combination in contrast to the static suburban lawn across the street.

Circulation: Moving Through Your Landscape

Walk your property to identify the high-use circulation routes. These are areas such as the walkway from the driveway to the front door or from the back porch to the garden shed. These high-use pathways are a good place to start as they highlight the areas you will see and pass through most often. Along these walks, note any features that catch your eye. This may be an attractive rock outcropping in the middle of your lawn or small pond in the corner of the yard.

Queues + Borrowed Views: Capitalizing on What Is Already There

Consider borrowed views from a neighbor's property such as a beautiful old tree with an attractive form. You may wish to "borrow" these features by siting your new meadow to strategically enhance these views. Also note any areas in need of improvement. Perhaps there is a large bare patch of grass, a neighbor's junk pile, or a muddy low point where the rainwater flows. See if there is a fence line with a stark transition to lawn that could be softened with a new planting. Be sure to capitalize on what is there already.

Consider the views from inside the house as well as in the landscape.

Front entries needn't be formal. This stoop is alive with texture, color, and inspiration.

Windows of Opportunity

Now go inside. Go to the windows that you look out of most often. Maybe this is your kitchen window over the sink or a large bay window across from the living room sofa. What views do these windows frame? Might there be an area you wish to enhance within these views? By selecting a location that you look at frequently, you will appreciate your creation more often.

Appealing to Your Neighbors

Another consideration is the view of your home from the street, referred to by real estate agents as curb appeal. Take time to assess yours and decide if your new meadow would be best sited where your neighbors can also enjoy it. Maybe you will inspire them to create their own. In this scenario, be sure to review your homeowners' association (HOA) rules regarding vegetation in the front yard.

A Little Help from Your Friends

Once you have walked your property and taken notes of the existing features, ask a friend or family member to do the same. Don't share your notes until they have made their own. Someone else's perspective will highlight the areas where you overlap, as well as point out items you may have missed. After each of you have a list of features, and before comparing, individually rank them in terms of prominence. Then discuss what you recorded and why you ranked them in the order that you did. Even though you are experiencing the same landscape, this will help you expand your perspective and offer insight that you may have overlooked on your own.

Soft gray, blue, and white complement this peaceful seating area, perfect for reflecting the moonlight.

Making a List of Possibilities + Recording Your Observations

Start a list of possible locations. Under each, begin to note the site conditions. For example, how many hours of sun does the area get? Remember to consider the time of year that you are doing the assessment. Do the light conditions change over the seasons as the trees leaf out? Does snow persist longer in certain locations such as on the north side of the house or under a large evergreen tree? While you may think rainfall would be consistent throughout your property, be sure to note locations such as roof overhangs, surface roots near large trees, soil compaction from foot or vehicular traffic, steep slopes where rainwater will shed quickly or erosion may occur, and low spots where rain will collect.

Additional Site Conditions

There is some initial research that you can do online, such as look up the average annual rainfall in your area. If you live in a place with winters, be sure to check the last frost date in the spring and first frost date in the fall. This is especially important if you are considering starting plants from seed or including annual species that may only survive in warmer temperatures.

Spotted beebalm (*Monarda punctata*) glows amongst the grasses. The subdued colors of these bracts last for weeks after the blooms have passed.

How to Do an At-Home Soil Test for Texture and pH

Try doing a simple soil texture test at home (sometimes called the squeeze test). This involves taking a small handful of soil from your site and squeezing it in your hand. If the soil falls apart when you open your hand, that means your soil is sandy. If it stays together, nudge it with your finger. If it remains together, that means you have clay soil. If it crumbles, that means you have loam. As soil textures are a continuum, it's probable that your soil is a combination or somewhere in between one of these three. This simple technique will give you a quick idea of what you are working with.

One of the reasons soil texture is important is that it will give you clues as to how quickly water will move through it. Sandy soil drains quickly—while clay soil drains more slowly. Loam is in between, meaning it retains some moisture without being water-logged.

Another factor to be aware of, as you get to know your site, is the soil pH. In general, this is usually something common among your region and easily determined by a quick internet search. If you would like to be more accurate, there are easy at-home pH test kits available via the mail or at your local garden center.

If you'd like a more comprehensive understanding of the texture, pH, and minerals on your site, many local government or educational agricultural agencies offer soil test results. They will give you instructions as to how to collect and submit a sample for analysis.

Use these tests to better understand your soil and help you with your plant selection.

Once you better understand the soil on your site, you can select a plant palette that will thrive in those conditions.

A painted lady butterfly feeding on a white coneflower.

Another element to consider is how the wind moves through your site. Where do the prevailing winds come from? When making notes on the possible locations you have selected, indicate whether they are protected from, or exposed to, desiccating winds. Also note where the existing wind breaks are located.

If you live in a mountainous area, knowing your elevation will help with plant selection. Plant lists will sometimes include elevations where a species is found in the wild. Something that grows well at a high elevation may struggle, or perform differently, at a lower elevation. It's important to know your general elevation and keep that in mind when pursuing plant lists for suggestions.

Your Goals Will Guide You

Now that you have inventoried and analyzed your property, you are ready to select a site. Consider your goals for this project. Are they purely aesthetic? Is there a view you would like to screen or enhance? Are you hoping to attract pollinators to your vegetable garden? Is there a failing, or underutilized, area of turf you wish to convert? Make a list of what you hope to achieve with your garden. In addition to your inventory and analysis, these goals will help to guide you to the best location.

Consider Your Time Commitment

Keep in mind the time you wish to devote to this project. Are there hurdles you will have to consider that will add to the labor? Perhaps there is a concrete pad that needs to be removed or an old stump and tree roots that need some attention before you can begin. Do you currently have the capacity to tackle this extra labor? Be sure to take this extra work into account. You may decide to begin somewhere that will take less time to prepare or you may wish to organize a brigade of friends and neighbors to help with the initial site preparation. Enlisting friends offers the opportunity to share your passion and hear about others' experiences while accomplishing more than you would on your own. Trade time and knowledge while collaborating with others.

Location Inspiration

What potential sites have you identified? Will you start small with a few large containers on a patio or balcony? Will you challenge yourself with a difficult location like an unirrigated hell strip between the sidewalk and the road? Is there a swale that directs water away from your foundation—fluctuating between being dry and inundated based on rainfall? Below we will explore the advantages and limitations of several possible locations.

Containers: Balcony, Stoop, Patio, or Rooftop

Pots and other containers are a simple way to experiment with creating a micro meadow. Whether it is one large pot or an assemblage of various sized pots, containers offer a unique option as site preparation will be minimal. You will be able to create your own soil by selecting a prepackaged container soil or mixing your own. It is important to get the growing media right in containers. As a rule, do not use topsoil or garden soil. These soils break down and compact over time, which reduces pore space, limiting proper air and soil drainage and water percolation.

As an artificial environment, this is one occasion where plant nutrition may require being managed by adding fertilizers and micronutrients. While you may add a percentage of compost to the initial mix, it is important to limit the overall ratio for the reasons listed above regarding compaction over time. Generally, when working in an existing garden bed, I select plants that will thrive in the existing soil conditions. Containers are an exception to that rule. You can include heavy feeders and supplement with fertilizers. Time-release fertilizers are one of the simplest solutions. If you have selected plants based on their flowers, be sure to choose a bloom-booster formulation. This will encourage more flowers.

The purple flowers and foliage of these sea holly contrast with the beiges and silver-blues of the grasses.

When designing a container planting, consider staging it first to imagine different layouts and combinations by mapping out the scale using tape or chalk.

If you live in an area that experiences winter, select hardy species that can tolerate the fluctuations in temperature that occur in soil that is not moderated by being below ground. You can also treat the planting as an annual installation. Another option is to move the container to a protected unheated space such as a garage—just be sure to add a little water periodically so it does not entirely dry out. If you suspect you will go this route, consider buying a heavy-duty pot caddy so that you can easily roll the planter to its offseason location. I recommend this for all larger containers so that they are elevated for good drainage and can be moved when necessary—while sparing your back.

Fence or Property Line

When it comes to property or fence lines, ask yourself if you want to call attention to them or blur them. What is adjacent? Is it a woodland or other natural area or an area with undesirable views? Maybe your lawn runs into the neighbor's lawn and makes your property feel more spacious. In this example, planting along the property line will disrupt the borrowed view and make your yard seem smaller. On the other hand, if you live next to a large natural area, you may wish to invite that view into your property by planting along the boundary and blurring the line between. If you have an existing fence, consider softening it by planting in front of it. Use the fence height as a gauge. If it is a six-foot (1.8 m) wooden fence, be sure the new bed is at least six feet (1.8 m) deep. A shallower planting will look like a decorative afterthought.

Front Walkway + Mailbox

Find a safe place to look at the front of your house from the street—maybe from your neighbor's sidewalk across the way. Find your front door and mailbox. How do you access them?

Do you have a front walkway that connects the driveway to the front door or the front door to the street? Is there a worn patch of turf showing the route you take to and from the mailbox every day? Do you enjoy a cup of tea on your front stoop in the mornings? Think of how you use your spaces. What area would you like to highlight or improve upon? For example, if you notice a worn path from daily foot traffic, maybe now is an opportunity to create something more permanent. Celebrate that pathway by creating something more deliberate with gravel, brick, or stone—creating a new garden opportunity.

Front walkways are interesting. Sometimes the front door is more of a formality than an actual high-use area. People will park cars in their garages or driveways and use a side entrance. Other times the front door is the primary access point to the house, so the walkway is used daily. Evaluate how you and your guests enter your house and how that relates to activity on your front walk. Always start with circulation. If your front walkway is used often, you will want to be generous with the space for circulation.

Perhaps you want to start small and experiment. Designing a planting area around or next to your mailbox is a way of creating a friendly welcome—for guests and postal workers alike. Prepare a garden bed at least as deep as the height of the mailbox. You may wish to select one or more taller species to place behind the box to ground it and soften the transition from the lawn, driveway, or sidewalk. One way that helps me decide the shapes and locations of beds is to look at how easy it will be to mow any adjacent turf. Eliminate small patches of grass that are hard to access to reduce future mowing and string trimming challenges.

The Hell Strip

For those unfamiliar with the term hell strip, it refers to the narrow patch of land between the

TOP Bringing the mailbox to life, a Monarch butterfly sips nectar from a bluebeard (*Caryopteris* sp.).

BOTTOM A narrow strip of soil along a fence line is all it takes to create a strip of meadow with a diversity of species.

sidewalk and the street. It is called this because it's a challenging space, but that's one of the reasons it's so fun to design. You will need to take into account limitations such as foot traffic, pets, poor soil, compaction, lack of irrigation, car pollution, road salt, and more. Provided you have a way to water a hell strip meadow during establishment, the poor quality of the soil and lack of irrigation make it an ideal location for many meadow and prairie plants. The density and informality of a naturalistic design add a layer of resiliency to a high traffic area.

When considering curb appeal, this is one of the first areas that guests and passers-by will see. While it's a high visibility area, it's often over-looked. Sometimes there will be lawn here, but typically it's a gravelly weed patch. Before you begin imagining the possibilities, check with local ordinances and any homeowners' association to see if there are restrictions governing this area.

You'll want to be familiar with any rules regarding planting there. If there is on-street parking, you'll need to plan for car doors opening and possible circulation through the strip. For example, if you have a walkway from the sidewalk to your front door, consider continuing that path through this area.

As circulation is a primary consideration, be sure the plants you select do not overhang the sidewalk. You will also want some form of edging to deter people and pets from stepping on the planting as it fills in. This can be something temporary like wooden stakes strung with rope—or something more permanent such as low metal fencing. Select hardy species that are tolerant of drought, pollution, and the occasional trampling. If you are limited for possible locations for your mini meadow, place it front and center for all to enjoy. Be the first on your street to activate this space and encourage your neighbors to follow.

OPPOSITE Often overlooked, this hell strip along a busy sidewalk is up for the challenge, thriving with minimal maintenance.

BELOW By including a large diversity of species and numerous planting methods, such as custom seed mixes and landscape plugs, resiliency is built into the design as site conditions change.

Veggie Garden or Raised Bed

With a renaissance in home vegetable gardening, people are reconnecting with growing their own food. It wasn't until I lived in a condo complex, without a yard of my own for the first time, that I discovered community gardening and began to experiment with growing my own food. A few blocks from where I lived, I was able to secure two small, raised beds for over three years. As I was new to growing food from seed on my own, I planted many different species and then waited to see what would come up in the spaces in between.

While food was my goal, I was fascinated with the pollinators that would visit my plots and dance from marigold seedling to cucumber blossom. In addition to welcoming volunteer flower seedlings into my allotments, I was asked to design a pollinator garden in a larger area to attract insects and other wildlife to this urban lot. I used a combination of seeds, plugs, and transplants. In time, I got as much pleasure from watching the diversity of bees and other insects as I did from eating a ripe organic heirloom tomato off the vine.

For smaller plots I recommend including flowering plants amongst the vegetable crops. If you have a larger vegetable garden or are part of

ABOVE Celebrate spontaneity by allowing meadow species to self-seed amongst the rows in your veggie plots.

OPPOSITE Food gardens can include flowering plants mixed directly amongst the vegetables, providing beauty and resources for pollinators and beneficial insects.

a community garden, you may consider devoting an entire area to a small pollinator meadow. When supporting pollinators and other insects, the simplest consideration is having a diversity of pollen and nectar over an extended period—from a diversity of blooms and overlapping flowering times throughout the seasons.

In this application, include plants that you can eat. Perhaps the flowers or leaves are edible and you can share them with bees and butterflies. See pages 154–155 for a chart of plant suggestions for an edible meadow. Customize your list with plants that thrive in your area. Ask friends and

neighbors what does well in their veggie gardens. As vegetables thrive on rich amended soil, the plants that will work here may be different that plants recommended for leaner unamended soils.

See if there are community gardens in your area. Visit a local organic farm and ask questions at your farmer's markets. Think about the layers of function and use that edible flowering plants play in attracting and supporting pollinators in a vegetable garden. Keep notes in your plant lists on their food/medicinal uses. Consider starting a column in your plant list for what insects visit the flowers.

A variety of warm- and cool-season grass and sedge species are used in this stormwater drainage system and were selected for their adaptability to the extreme conditions of drought and periodic inundation.

Rain Garden or Drainage Swale

Rain is a precious and often overlooked resource. In some areas there is an abundance. In these locations you may be tasked with guiding it away from foundations and other structures or directing it to retention or detention areas. In most single-family residential settings this would include a bioswale or rain garden.

Here is an opportunity to design a meadow that can tolerate being inundated for short periods as well as potentially being dry for extended periods. Native wetland plants are a good place to start when creating your plant list. Also consider the location of where the species will be planted. Certain plants are best for the low parts of the swale or rain garden that stay wet the longest and others are better for the middle and upper edges that stay wet for a shorter time.

This unique environment allows you to expand your planting palette beyond other areas of your property. You will be able to work with plants that are found along streambanks and beside ponds and lakes. Create a list of possible species that will work in these conditions and that match the aesthetic you are trying to achieve. Keep in mind that you may wish to contact a professional if taking on any extensive regrading or redirection of water. They can help you with the calculations to determine the size and depth of the swale or rain garden.

Seaside + Coast

Coastal areas have to contend with salt, in the air and soil, desiccating winds, and sharp drainage due to a high sand/gravel content in the soil. When considering a coastal location for your new meadow, be sure to select plant species that are adapted to these conditions. Locate the direction of the prevailing winds and consider planting taller hardy species (including grasses) toward the back to screen the new planting. You will have to monitor young plants to establish the watering requirements. Watering may be more frequent than you expect due to the drainage, breezes, and salt.

There are many plant species that thrive in coastal locations so you will have plenty from which to choose. As mentioned in other sections, I recommend selecting the right plants for the site conditions verses amending the site in an attempt to include less tolerant species. Often coastal and other wetland areas have setbacks and buffer zones that need to be taken into consideration. Be sure you familiarize yourself with any codes and regulations in your area.

The sea lavender (Limonium sp.) and grasses have adapted to tolerate the salt spray, wind, and occasional flooding of the shoreline.

Meadows are not just for full sun locations. There are many woodland flowering plants that combine well to create a meadow in part shade. Select a location with dappled shade or under deciduous (leaves fall off in winter) trees. The shade cast by evergreen trees or that is found on the north side of a house or other structure is too dense for a showy mixed flower display. While there are plants that will grow here, it is not ideal for a meadow so you may wish to consider other options.

For deep shade, your selection will be limited, but you can still create a full shade interpretation of a meadow, albeit with fewer flowers. Plants that require full sun need six hours or more of direct sunlight. Part shade means four to six hours of sun and full shade is less than four hours. Many species are flexible and will tolerate a range of sunlight—but most will have a preference where they perform best.

You may wish to limb up the surrounding vegetation to let in more light. Evaluate this prior to planting your new garden. In sunnier locations, warm- and cool-season grasses can provide the texture and background for a meadow. In the shade, there are many sedge (*Carex*) and rush (*Juncus*) options to explore that will perform well with less sun.

Another textural favorite of mine to include are ferns. While there are some ferns that will tolerate sun, most prefer shadier conditions. If you decide to site your new meadow in the shade, celebrate this unique opportunity to add the distinctive foliage of fern species to the mix. See pages 156–157 in chapter seven for a list of suggested part-shade favorites.

The lacy foliage of maidenhair fern (*Adiantum pedatum*) and the coarser broad fronds of sensitive fern (*Onoclea sensibilis*) weave together around a patch of jack-in-the-pulpit (*Arisaema triphyllum*).

Borrowed or Shared Land

Are you short on outdoor space at your condo or apartment? Check to see if there are community gardens in your area. While these landscapes are usually focused on growing food, it may be possible to establish a pollinator meadow or cut flower meadow to share with wildlife and other gardeners. Is there a nearby public park, abandoned lot, traffic median, or other space that could use an upgrade? Chat with your neighbors, and your local

representatives, about creating a mini meadow on borrowed land for all to enjoy. Think of it as an "adopt a spot." In Providence, Rhode Island, United States of America, the city teamed up with a land trust to transform vacant lots into urban gardens. You don't need much space to create a colorful and thriving mini meadow. Working the land with your friends and neighbors fosters community and will inspire others to do the same.

From a small hillside on a woodland edge (ABOVE) to a large container planting (LEFT), experiment at a scale that feels comfortable to you. This makes it easier to correct your mistakes and expand upon your successes.

Start Small + Remember Your Goals

You have now completed a thorough site assessment and made a list of possible locations for your project. Have you decided where you would like to site your new garden? If this is your first time designing a meadow and you have a couple of possibilities, I recommend selecting the smallest area with the least amount of preparation to begin experimenting. Once you've become more familiar with the process, you can expand to other locations. Now that you better understand your site, use the information you gained from the inventory and analysis to begin designing your new garden. Refer back to your list of goals as guidance. These steps and details are essential in creating a successful project and the extra effort upfront will make your life easier in the long run.

3

Designing Your Mini Meadow

Function and Aesthetics Combine to Create the Perfect Meadow Planting

You've found inspiration, selected your site, and are now ready to begin designing. Using the observations made in the previous chapter regarding the conditions of your space, you will now begin to put together a plan along with a list of your favorite plant species. Depending on your level of expertise, and the complexity of the project, this can be a simple bubble diagram with rough dimensions or a scaled drawing. It is important to know the overall size of the space you will be using so you know the approximate number of plants you will need.

Keep in mind the list of goals you created in the last chapter. Is this garden purely aesthetic? Are you looking to screen something? Do you want to attract certain insects like butterflies or bees? These questions will further inform your plant selection and design as you move forward. For the plant selection, start with a brainstorm.

Refer to any lists you may have started from nature walks or preliminary research. Create a master list of possibilities and include all the plants that excite you. You will refine this later, but for now, let your imagination run wild.

Let's review the steps to design and plan a garden:

Designing and planning steps completed
- Inventory and analysis
- Select a site
- Set your goals

Next steps
- Make a base plan
- Calculate the number of plants needed
- Make a corresponding plant list
- Consider the essential design elements
- Create a planting plan or strategy

Rattlesnake master (*Eryngium yuccifolium*), white coneflower (*Echinacea purpurea* 'White Swan'), and muhly grass (*Muhlenbergia reverchonii*) combine well, both regarding aesthetic as well as their preference for similar growing conditions.

Making a Base Plan

The next step in the design process after a thorough inventory and analysis of your site is to create a base plan. In its simplest form, a base plan will give you the overall dimensions of a space. You may also wish to note certain site conditions and features that you inventoried. This can be a simple napkin sketch or a bubble diagram on graph paper.

How to Measure

You will need to take measurements of the area and site features you wish to include. There are a few ways to accomplish this. Start with a quick sketch of the areas and features you'd like to measure. Because you will just be using this sketch to record the measurements, it needn't be proportionate. Then decide how you'd like to go about measuring.

A base plan helps you visualize the overall dimension of the space, including site conditions and features you recorded during your inventory.

Steps + Paces

The two simplest ways to get rough dimensions are steps and paces. To use the steps method, measure your shoe from end to end. Then walk the length you'd like to measure—placing the heel of your shoe directly in front of the toe of your other foot. Count the number of steps and multiply this by the length of your shoe.

For larger areas, measure by paces. As paces vary from person to person, you will first need to determine the length of your pace. Measure a given distance with a tape measure—say one hundred feet (30.5 meters). Then count the paces it takes you to walk it. Divide one hundred (or 30.5 meters) by that number. For example, if it took you twenty-five paces, you know that your pace measures roughly four feet (1.2 meters). I use both methods to gather measurements quickly.

Tape Measure + Measuring Wheel

For more precise measurements, use a tape measure or measuring wheel. The easiest way to use a tape measure is with a partner to hold one end. If the tape is not long enough for the distance you are measuring, use an object like a stick, rock, or flag to mark where you left off and continue from that point. If you are measuring solo, be sure the tape measure has a functional lock. It will take a bit more time walking back and forth, but it will be just as accurate as having an assistant. If you are planning to take measurements of your entire property, consider investing in a measuring wheel. These collapsible wheels take quick measurements and are easy to use one-handed. Both the measuring tape and measuring wheel provide more accurate numbers than the steps or pacing methods.

Napkin Sketch

A napkin sketch might literally be on a napkin. It's a term used to describe a quick sketch that captures the essence of a design. I recommend starting here to let your ideas flow before concerning yourself with dimensions. You will make several iterations, so keep it quick and gestural. Once you've drawn something you like, note the overall dimensions for reference as well as any existing conditions that will influence your design.

For larger areas, consider using a measuring wheel, which is easy to use with one hand.

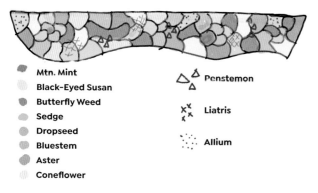

Mtn. Mint
Black-Eyed Susan
Butterfly Weed
Sedge
Dropseed
Bluestem
Aster
Coneflower

Penstemon

Liatris

Allium

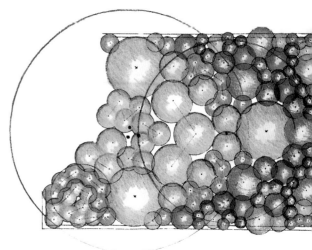

Planting plans can be as simple as using color and/or patterns to identify a plant species and various circle or bubble sizes to approximate a plant's mature size. You can digitally draw your plants (LEFT) or hand-draft them (RIGHT).

Graph Paper

A bubble diagram is also a loose sketch. If you use graph paper, assigning a dimension to the squares will result in a more accurate depiction of the existing space. This will help you lay out the garden proportionally without worrying too much about being exact. You can focus only on the planting site or include more of the surrounding areas for context such as the building, driveway, or lawn adjacent to your planting.

Using the largest dimension of the area you wish to capture, determine what scale will fit your paper. There are many formats of graph paper in terms of how many squares per page. Will one square equal one foot (30 cm)? If it's a small area, will four squares equal one foot (30 cm)? You may also tape two or more sheets together for a larger plan.

Mapping It Out on Paper

I find it easiest to start with a pencil, a good eraser, and some kind of straight-edge ruler or substitute. Begin with the largest overall dimension and measure it on the paper making dots with a sharpened pencil. Then, map out the next overall dimension. For example, if your largest measurement is the width, follow that with the length. Be sure the overall area fits on the paper you have selected. Now, using your straightedge, connect the dots. If your area is not a square, repeat the original steps until you've laid out the overall outside dimensions of your space. Again, don't worry about being perfect. It will take a few tries to become comfortable with these steps and your accuracy will improve with practice.

If your base plan focuses solely on your new garden site, lay out any additional site features within that area. Once completed, you will have a base plan on which to begin laying out your planting design. If you've chosen to include adjacent areas or the whole property, you will need to continue taking measurements and laying them out on your page. I recommend using pencil until you have the majority of measurements worked out. Even with practice, it is important to be able to make adjustments as you go.

Additional Drafting Supplies

In addition to a pencil, eraser, and straight edge, you will need a variety of permanent marker sizes. I use ultra-fine point, fine point, and chisel tip markers for simple drawings. I also use a white out correction pen. I use the ultra-fine point marker for the smaller details such as plant material. The large chisel tip can be used for buildings and property lines and the fine point for intermediate details such as paths. Whatever you choose to include, create a hierarchy using line weights (thickness of the markers) to help guide your eye.

A simplest sketch will capture the planting area. A more involved base plan will include adjacent areas or even the entire property. As a landscape designer, I encourage clients to consider the overall property and to take into account the relationships between areas. For this book we will continue to focus on smaller plantings, but some readers may wish to "zoom out" and include more when creating their base plan.

Calculating the Number of Plants Needed

Note your overall square footage by multiplying the length times the width and then subtract out any areas that will not be planted, such as paths or seating areas. For irregular-shaped gardens, estimate the area by dividing the project into simple shapes like triangles and rectangles. Determine the square footage of these smaller sections and add them together to get the total. At this point you will have enough information to determine a rough number of plants needed to complete your design.

For meadow plantings I estimate one plant per square foot or one foot on center (from center of plant to center of plant). In metric, this is one plant per 0.09 m² or 30 cm on center. Depending on the species you choose, your actual plant placement will vary from six inches to two feet (15–60 cm) on center. One foot (30 cm) on center works as an average. Exceptions to this would be container plantings or a design using only annuals. In these cases where plants will be placed even closer, use smaller spacing such as nine inches (23 cm) or tighter.

Using one plant per square foot (0.09 m²) as an estimate, determine your overall square footage and multiply by 1 to get the approximate number of plants you will need. When planting at nine inches (23 cm) on center, multiply the square footage by 1.8 to get the number of plants required.

If you will be using a combination of seeds and plants, you will need to massage these calculations to suit your specific ratios. For example, if you are planning for one plant per square foot (0.09 m²), but you will be installing them half as containerized plants and half as seed, you would multiply your total square footage by 0.5 to determine the total number of plants needed of each type for your project.

Revisiting Your Goals

As we touched upon in the last chapter, it is critical to consider your goals during this process and to refer back to them often. A goal may be as simple as beautifying a certain area. Setting clear goals will help you as you continue your research. For example, if you are looking to support pollinators, select a plant palette that includes a continuation of blooms throughout the seasons. In this case, include a column in your plant list with bloom times. I find it helpful to identify a few sources for reliable plant information in your area and to stick to these when researching each species. You can find plant suggestions and sample lists along with additional information to include in your own list in chapter seven.

Additional research will depend on the goals and site conditions you have identified. This may include wetland species for rain gardens or tall sturdy plants for privacy or windbreaks. Perhaps you live close to the coast or your garden area is close to a road that gets salted in the winter. You will need to create a list of plants that are tolerant of these conditions.

Other goals may include attracting certain insect or bird species. You may wish to research larval host plants for butterflies or certain color plants to attract hummingbirds. Maybe your garden area will be next to an outdoor kitchen or patio where you gather in the evening. In this case, consider planting white flowering species to shine in the moonlight or edible species to include in your salads or cocktail. Whatever your objectives are, brainstorming and identifying them before you begin designing improves the overall outcome. Doing so allows you to be more intentional about your site and plant selections—and the overall design.

Making a Plant List

You have now established a base plan and know approximately how many plants to include in your new meadow. Your goals and site conditions have helped to define your search criteria. Your inspiration from the wild and designed spaces you have visited will further inform your selection. Plant list creation is covered later in this chapter and in chapter seven. We're touching upon it here, so you know how to get started. The plants are the major players in your design process and the overall success of your project.

Keep an open mind. Start with a brainstorm list of words that you want your new planting to exude—and then pick your top three to five. Do you want a loud, riotous, colorful planting in fiery warm tones? Do you want a soothing planting with cool colors that inspire calm? Take notes on what you intend to create. This will help to direct your focus amongst the many choices you'll encounter.

Many plant lists are already available to help guide you. Search on the internet using words that describe your site. Be sure to include your region. For example, you could search for "drought tolerant, full sun, perennials, Frankfurt, Germany" or "native, salt tolerant, grasses, San Diego, California." See what lists of plants your searches generate. Then, conduct an image search by botanical name to see if the plants appeal to you. Also refer to the sample lists in chapter seven starting on page 140.

Collecting Images for Inspiration

You may also wish to keep a digital or paper folder of design inspiration photos. It is important to include images that show the plants in context with other species. While close-up glamour shots of specific flowers are beautiful, they won't help you to understand how the plants interact in a design. Select images that evoke feelings.

Look for plant combinations that call to you based on their textures and colors. Find pictures that show gardens at various times of the year so you can begin to consider how they will change over the course of the seasons. These images will be a place from which to begin dreaming and also a reposit to circle back to when you need to center your imagination and clarify your intentions.

Starting a List of Your Own

Taking into account the scale of your new meadow, begin to make a list of plant species you wish to include. Refer to chapter seven as to how to set up your chart, what columns and information to include, and what notes to take. You will

This Monarch butterfly rests on the stem of a Rudbeckia seedhead as the Monarch migrates south.

refine the list in the next step, but for now, cast a wide net. Get your favorites on the page. This master list will be useful for future expansions or other designs.

Creating a well-researched plant list is critical to the success of the design and project. Meadow gardens are loose, but there are patterns and repetition. Avoid creating a collector's garden with one of every species that thrills you from trips to the nursery without your list. This is not to say there is no room for experimentation. If something catches your eye, but you are unfamiliar with the species, or your growing conditions are outside the recommendations for that plant, try one and see how it does.

TOP Here is a newly planted meadow in mid-summer with a diversity of flowering perennials, self-seeding annuals, and a mixture of warm- and cool-season grasses.

BOTTOM The same planting four months later in late autumn. While the colors have shifted, the design remains interesting and cohesive even without flowers.

Narrowing It Down

Once you have a good list of plant choices, begin to research them to determine if they are right for your site and design. Don't be afraid to use the botanical names as this will ensure you are learning about the correct species. Keep two to three trusted resources handy that include the species on your list.

Your goals and site conditions will guide this process. Be intentional. The site limitations you've established will help narrow down your plant choices. Once you have researched all of the plants on your master list, copy all of the species that are a good match to a new list. Those that are ill-suited can be saved for future projects in other locations. If there are a couple of species that are questionable, include them in your list with an asterisk. When you begin designing, plan to use these questionable plants in smaller quantities until you know how they perform in your new garden.

Review your new list. Is there enough variety? Do you have too many choices? If you have more species than you think you will use, continue to refine your list by moving your favorites to the top. Don't eliminate possible good candidates until after you have confirmed you can source your top choices. Remember to keep it simple. The next section will introduce topics that will help you to better understand how to use the species you have selected to create a beautiful design.

Checking-In on the Process

How are you feeling about the design process so far? If you're anxious to get started, you may wish to experiment in the field. Once you have established the rough square footage and number of plants needed, you could go directly to your local nursery and purchase plants. Annuals (plants that live for only one year or season) are especially forgiving because you'll get to redesign the meadow every year. Winging it is certainly one way to familiarize yourself with the process. There is nothing wrong with just going for it! However, I suspect if you purchased this book, you are looking for more guidance and would prefer to take a more informed approach.

The opposite of jumping right in is overanalyzing to the point of paralysis. There are thousands of choices and near limitless combinations. Each species can be researched and cross-checked with multiple sources. You can make extensive lists and charts—cataloging all the notes and information you collect. If this is one of your first planting designs, my advice would be to start simple. Experiment with a large container or small planting area. Familiarize yourself with the inventories at your local plant nurseries. Remember to ask questions and take notes when you visit. Assemble enough knowledge to make informed choices while still moving your project forward in a timeline that allows you to enjoy it in the coming weeks or months.

Unlike the more drought-tolerant species on the opposite page, scarlet beebalm (*Monarda didyma*) performs best in rich, moist, well-drained soil. It is critical to know your site conditions and select your plant palette accordingly.

Essential Design Elements to Consider

Before we jump into creating a planting plan and strategy, it's important to touch on some essentials of good design. The following sections include design elements to consider when you are approaching your new project. These include simple broad-brush introductory considerations such as color, layers, textures, and seasonality. Each will help you better understand what to be thinking about as you daydream and design.

Right Plant, Right Place

The adage "right plant, right place" is an important one. It means you must know about the needs of the plants you are including and about the site

OPPOSITE This fiery mix of warm-toned coneflowers (*Echinacea purpurea* var.), butterfly milkweed (*Asclepias tuberosa*), red hot poker (*Kniphofia* sp.), red Mexican hat plant (*Ratibida columnifera forma pulcherrima*), and yellow lilies (*Lilium* sp.) creates visual harmony by employing analogous colors, those found next to each other on the color wheel.

you have selected. Rather than try to amend your site to suit the needs of the species you'd like to use, it's best to select plants that suit your site. Take the information gathered in your inventory and analysis and use it to determine what types of plants are best matched to the conditions.

For example, if you are planting in a coastal location in full sun with no automatic irrigation system, you will want to only consider species that love those conditions. While many plants are sold as drought-tolerant, it is important to note that all new installations may require initial supplemental watering during establishment. If on the other hand, your site is in dappled shade at the bottom of a hill where the rainwater collects, you'll want to limit your search to species that thrive in damp partial-shade. These constraints help to focus your plant search. Be clear about the site conditions and know the preferred growing conditions of the plants. This will save you time and money, as well as will result in a more successful project over time.

Keep It Simple

When designing a new garden, especially a small space as a new gardener, simplicity is key. It may be that you only choose to work with a handful of plant species and that's okay! Even if your space is a little larger, repeating a small number of species may be ideal. Keeping the palette simple will make the design more readable. You can select one of each species for smaller applications or multiples of each for larger areas. Grasses and grass-like plants will form the foundation of your garden. Even if you are attracted to the flowering aspect of meadows, grasses are a quintessential element that will tie the design together—creating texture and movement even when there is nothing in bloom as well as root your design in a meadow identity.

Similar to the goals section, consider how you will use the space. Will this be a garden that you gaze upon from the kitchen window or a planting you pass through on your way to the mailbox? Will you meander amongst the plants on your way to your favorite bench? Is this meadow primarily for you and your family, for visitors and passers-by, for wildlife, or all of the above? If it's for you and you've decided to create it in your backyard, you have full freedom to experiment with whatever you like. If, on the other hand, this new planting will be viewed from the street with the potential to inspire your neighbors, consider a little restraint and circle back to simplicity.

Pathways

A meadow that you will meander through needs a pathway of some kind. It could be fieldstone stepping stones, crushed gravel, existing turf, or something more formal like brick or flagstone. Meandering is a slow exploratory pace. That means the path can be narrow and even have small plants speckled in it that you will step over or around.

A planting you will pass through suggests you will be moving at a faster pace. This may be a primary walkway such as from the driveway to the front porch. In this case, make a wider path and keep the plantings low that are close to it. You may be carrying bags of groceries or pushing a stroller and will appreciate the clearance. Either way, you will want some height to the plantings so that they envelop you. This can be the suggestion of height through the use of an occasional tall plant or something more defined like drifts of grasses (groupings set out in an informal way).

Pathways lead the eye through a garden (NEAR RIGHT) as well as offer a way to move through a planting and experience it from within (OPPOSITE).

Color

In many ways color is a personal preference. However, there are certain combinations that read more successfully. Some people have an innate sense of color harmony (visually pleasing color combinations). If you don't fit that category, consult a color wheel.

There are primary colors (red, yellow, and blue), secondary colors (orange, green, and purple), and tertiary colors (combinations thereof such as blue-green or yellow-green). In order to achieve color harmony, you want to make combinations that are neither too bland, nor too chaotic. **Analogous colors** appear next to each other on the color wheel. Examples of analogous colors are red-orange, orange, and orange-yellow. **Complementary colors** are those directly opposite each other on the color wheel. Examples of complementary colors are yellow and purple or yellow-green

and purple-red. Colors will read, or appear, differently depending on how they are paired.

Be aware of these terms and consult the color wheel if you have questions. When applying color theory to your mini meadow design, first decide if you have a favorite color or group of colors you wish to include. Then decide if you'd like to work with analogous or complementary colors to accompany your dominant color(s). This color palette will help to narrow your search. Keep in mind that different species bloom at different times. It's important to consider estimated bloom times so you know what colors will be present at any given moment.

Often, I will start with selecting either **warm** (red, orange, and yellow) or **cool** (green, blue, and purple) tones as the overarching color theme. If most of the flowers will be cool, I may then select

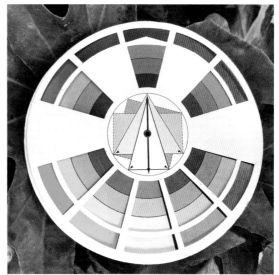

Analogous colors appear next to each other on the color wheel (ABOVE). While the opposite left photo leans warm with the pinks of the Joe-Pye weed and *Agastache*, the opposite right photo is cool with the purple of the garden sage, 'Caradonna' meadow sage, and blue iris. The left photo includes the early season cool-colored foliage of daffodils, muhly grass, lupine, and 'Husker Red' penstemon.

a couple of species that contrast with the predominant cool color. Here the color palette will be harmonious because I have selected mostly analogous colors but have added a bit of drama with the contrasting pop provided by one or two warm-colored plants. An example would be blue and purple flowers, paired with the green tones of the foliage. I would then select some orange or red-orange flowers to provide contrast. If you are just beginning, remember to *keep it simple*.

Color is not just about flowers either. There is a whole spectrum of green from yellow-green to green-blue. The foliage of plants is also an important component as it exists even when the plants are not in bloom. Foliage comes in almost every color these days. In addition to green, there are blue-, gray-, yellow-, white-, purple-, pink-, and even black-leaved plants to name a few. As a rule,

I avoid yellow foliage plants. They tend to call too much attention to themselves and don't play harmoniously with others.

Generally, I stick to green foliage unless I am going all in on a theme. If I decide to use foliage other than green, I will usually select multiple analogous foliage colors. For example, if I have decided to use purple foliage, I will select multiple purple foliage plants and then decide if I want to incorporate warm or cool colors for the accompanying foliage. For cool colors I may include black-, gray-, and/or blue-leaved plants. For warmer colors I may use pink, magenta, and red-purple foliage. While there are many different colored foliage plants on the market today, I caution people away from using most of them. Stick to the greens and blue-grays found in nature or go all in with a playful saturated colorful foliage scheme.

ABOVE Joe-Pye weeds (*Eutrochium* sp.) emerge from the lower skullcap (*Scutellaria* sp.) layer.

OPPOSITE *Echinacea*, *Berlandiera*, and *Rudbeckia* tuck into the foliage below the flower spikes of *Agastache*. Plains zinnia fill the gaps at the bases of the taller plants.

Layers

Layering is how plants are arranged on the vertical plane. A forest is a good example. There are tall canopy trees, understory trees, bushes, herbaceous plants, and groundcovers. Layering also occurs within each of these types. A meadow is made up of predominantly herbaceous plants (forbs and grasses that die back to the ground over winter). The simplified layers of a meadow planting include the tall structural species, the medium fill plants, and the lower groundcover plants.

Layering is important for several reasons. First, layering creates complex visual interest. Not only is there the static image of how a planting looks today, but also the dynamic temporal layering of how plants emerge, fill in, and wither over time. Secondly, dense layering will reduce your maintenance by shading out weed species. The less there is of open ground available for seeds to germinate, the less weeding chores you will encounter. The term "green mulch" is used to describe low-growing plants that cover the ground beneath the showier middle and upper layers. Third, layering offers diverse habitat, shelter, and forage to wildlife—attracting more species to your garden.

While there is no perfect formula, I target for a ratio of one quarter taller structural species, one half mid-height plants, and one quarter ground-cover species. Within each of these sections are further layers. Specific height ranges will depend on the scale of your project and the species you choose to include. For a diverse meadow planting, I would say tall structural species are those over thirty inches (76 cm) and low groundcover species are those under twelve inches (30 cm). The middle

Sprays of lavender-blue meadow sage (*Salvia pratensis*) hover above the lower layer of cushion spurge (*Euphorbia polychrome*) and lady's-mantle (*Alchemilla mollis*), both soon to bloom in contrasting yellows.

The fine foliage and small flowers of this Mexican hat plant (*Ratibida columnifera forma pulcherrima* and *forma columnifera*) look best en masse, making it a candidate for the seasonal drift category.

layer is anything in between. However, these are just suggestions that will vary with each project.

Further delineation may be made within each of these layers. In the **tallest layer** where certain plants emerge above the rest, it is important to keep architecture in mind. While some of the species you select may be diffuse or delicate, you want to keep the focus on strong silhouettes. Think of them as the sculptures of the planting. *Echinacea purpurea* (purple coneflower) and *Eutrochium* (formerly *Eupatorium*) spp. (Joe-pye weed) are good examples. The *Echinacea* dances above the surrounding plants both in flower and seed. The *Eutrochium* towers above in a column of bold foliage with purple-pink flat-topped umbels. Species such as these will punctuate the masses of the lower layers.

The **mid-layer** range is a bit of a catch all for those plants that are neither the tallest nor the shortest. Within this layer are seasonal drifts, architectural plants, and intermixed species (or matrix plants). **Seasonal drifts** are those groupings that make their impact while flowering but lack strong foliage or much interest when not in bloom. Generally, perennials do not flower for long periods. It's important to identify those species that you'd like to include just for their seasonal blooms, so you place them accordingly—typically en masse.

As with the tallest layer, **architectural plants** are those with a distinctive structure that helps them to stand out from others—in and out of flower. **Intermixed or matrix layer** plants are species that play well in mixed groups. Instead of blocks or drifts of single species, these are drifts of various species that are repeated. They have more structure than the seasonal drifts but not so much as to stand out strongly like the architectural plants.

Finally, there is the **groundcover layer**. This can be made up of low spreading plants and short clumping plants. Due to their small size, group

Adrift in a sea of muhly grass (*Muhlenbergia reverchonii* UNDAUNTED), *Kniphofia*, goldenrod, *Erigeron*, sea holly, and tall verbena shine in the afternoon sun.

Drifts of *Amsonia* weave through this rooftop planting, creating a place for the eye to rest amongst the intermixed plantings and guiding the visitor along the path.

low clumping species so they read well. Place spreading groundcovers individually or in groups and encourage them to ramble around the bases of the taller layers. Understanding the growing habits of these shorter species will help you when designing the layout and deciding how many of each are needed. The important thing to remember with this last layer is to fill in the gaps and cover the ground. Like a living mulch, these species help to prevent weed infiltration by shading out potential weed seeds. They also help to retain moisture and provide valuable habitat for insects and other small wildlife.

Massing + Matrices

Depending on the scale of your meadow, you may be using multiples of each species that you have selected. In this case there are many different ways to lay out your plants. Some of the basic techniques

OPPOSITE When backlit, it is easy to see how taller species such as rattlesnake master (*Eryngium yuccifolium*) become architectural additions to a planting.

include massing and matrices. Massing is the simplest form. Here you design the plants in groups, usually by species or sometimes by color. I use odd numbers in my groupings. You may lay out all of the same species together or you may lay them out in smaller groups and repeat those smaller groupings throughout the planting. Massing can occur in distinctive blocks or more diffuse drifts that fade into their neighbors. While blocks may have hard transitions between one species and the next, drifts tend to intermingle where they meet and are generally more freeform than blocks.

Matrix (or intermixed) planting involves grouping various plant species together based on similar textures and heights. These plants tend to have less visual impact than the architectural plant layers described previously. The matrix plants form the foundation layer for the showier structural plants and seasonal drifts. Group them in terms of height. This can be as simple as low, mid-, and tall matrix groups. The matrices can also be laid out in blocks or drifts. I find it easiest to establish where the architectural plants go first, followed by the seasonal drifts, and lastly the matrices.

Texture

Texture is another important area to consider as you design. As mentioned, grasses are a foundation layer to any meadow. Grasses and grass-like plants provide verticality and movement. Overlapping and weaving together, they're also an essential component for winter interest, as well as for providing mating and nesting habitat for birds and other wildlife. Dramatic in their subtly, they sometimes take center stage and other times are the backdrop on which the flowers pop.

Grasses come in a variety of forms—from fine and narrow to fat and strappy. Be sure to select a variety so that there is a balance. Just as too many different bold colors can be chaotic, so too can too many bold leaf shapes. The opposite is also true. Using too many plants with delicate foliage can look messy or lack interest. Balance occurs when large leaves punctuate the finer-textured foliage.

One technique I have tried is to take a photo of a plant assemblage and to convert it to black and white. Looking at the image, is the combination interesting? Does it read well? Does your eye move comfortably through the design? Try this with your phone camera at the nursery with the plants in your cart and repeat it in your garden once the plants have begun to establish.

Seasonality, Time + Life Cycles

Another consideration as you research and design your mini meadow is seasonality and the life cycles of the plants you choose. Gardens are ever-changing through the seasons, over the

TOP The upright seedheads of the cool season prairie junegrass (*Koeleria macrantha*) stand out amongst the airy sprays of prairie dropseed (*Sporobolus heterolepis*) in this simple grass matrix.

BOTTOM The fine textures of the agastache and sedge contrast with the bold palm-like leaves of the lupine.

As summer greens fade to the tans and browns of fall, late-blooming flowers mingle with the seed heads of neighboring grasses and perennials.

course of years, and even throughout the day. This fourth dimension of time is one of the things that delighted me about landscape and planting design. Gardens as works of art are not static like a painting and won't repeat themselves in an identical way like viewing a film.

For wildlife and visual interest alike, it is important to understand how your meadow will change over the seasons as well as from year to year. Herbaceous plants are either annual (living for one year), biennial (living for two years), short-lived perennial (regrowing every year for a few years), and perennial (coming back for many years). I use annual, biennial, and perennial as designations for the "type" of plant in my plant lists. I can then sort the lists based on how long the plants will persist.

You may wish to design a meadow filled with **annuals**. This will result in flower color during the first growing season. Annuals tend to be less expensive than perennial plants—especially when they are sold in four or six-packs or as flats. The trade-off is that you will need to purchase plants each spring. Some annuals are strong self-seeders. We get into more detail on self-seeding and volunteer plants in chapter six.

I often use young **perennial** plants in my designs—sold as either plugs or in small pots. Young perennials may not bloom in their first, or even second, year. To bring color during that time, I include a percentage of annuals—typically, annuals that I know will reseed. As the perennial plants begin to establish, these self-seeding annuals will volunteer in the voids between the more permanent plants. You will be surprised by how quickly a young perennial plant will fill in. Buying young plants helps to stretch the budget, allowing for more plants. It is also important to note if the perennials you have selected are short-lived or not. As this will vary by location, try to source regional information as to how each species performs in your area.

There are many beautiful plants that may only last three to five years. These short-lived perennials differ from biennials. A **biennial** completes its life cycle in two years. In my experience, they tend to spend their first-year photosynthesizing and producing foliage. In the second year, they flower and go to seed. If any of the species you have selected are biennial, and you'd like to have them blooming every year, you'll want to plant young plants each season—at least until they've begun self-seeding and appearing on their own.

Continuous Blooms

In addition to ensuring the flowers you like will bloom every year, you also want to aim for a continuity of blooms throughout the year. Include a column in your plant list for bloom time. Once planted, keep track of when each species blooms in your garden. If you notice there are periods of time where nothing is blooming, look for a species that will fill those gaps. For early spring, consider bulbs to extend the bloom time earlier in the season. Depending on the climate where you live, you may be able to have something in flower year-round. If you have cold winters where all the plants die back, be sure to select some species

Self-seeding annuals such as these *Rudbeckia*, *Verbena*, and *Gomphrena* find their way into pockets between the warm season grasses.

that have strong architectural interest in their foliage and seed heads. See more about winter interest on page 130.

Creating a Planting Plan or Strategy

Now that you've been introduced to some design consideration basics, you're ready to start imagining how you'll apply them to your space. You can do so either by creating a planting plan or a planting strategy. A planting plan can be simple or complex—a rough sketch or a careful detailed drawing. For our purposes as beginners, let's explore a simple sketch.

If you decided to create a base plan, layer trace paper over it and get started. A roll of trace paper is inexpensive. The best way to learn is to just begin. Trace paper allows you to crumple it up and start again as you work through the process of putting your ideas on paper. Once you have begun to create something you like, continue to layer trace paper on top to further refine your drawing. Repeat this until you are satisfied with the results.

You may use bubbles to represent masses of certain species or groups of mixed plantings. Different patterns, symbols, shapes, or even colors can represent different plants. The point is to work out your ideas and the relationships each plant or plant mass has to one another. As you will most likely be installing the design your-self, only you need to understand your drawing. This gives you even more freedom to let loose and work through your design. You know from

establishing the square footage of your space roughly how many plants will be included. The planting plan forces you to take a closer look. You will have another opportunity to reevaluate the design as you lay the plants out in the field prior to installation.

A planting strategy is even more loose than a planting plan. You may use the exercise of creating a plan to help you create a strategy or vice versa. Rather than the exact location of each plant, a strategy is more about how you will lay out the plants during installation. It asks you to consider how the plants you have selected fit into the various design considerations mentioned earlier—especially the layers component. Sort your plant list by height and group different ranges together such as emergent, mid-, and low groundcover. Ultimately, the exercise forces

Moon carrot (*Seseli gummiferum*) is a standout biennial and pollinator magnet for dry, sandy soils.

The same first-year meadow strip planting two months apart: end of July (RIGHT) end of September (BELOW).

Visit your local nurseries to explore their stock and display gardens, meet their staff, and ask questions.

Mail-order plants often ship bareroot or in small pots. It's especially important to keep these small plants watered and cared for until they are installed.

greater observation and analysis so that you arrange your planting in an aesthetically pleasing way. One possibility is that your strategy may be to have no strategy at all!

Sourcing Plants

Another aspect to keep in mind as you create your plant list and begin designing is plant availability. You may have found a certain species on a walk or seen a specific cultivar in a magazine that you would like to include that is not available in your area or in the trade in general. Sourcing adds another filter to your design process.

Support Your Local Nurseries

First, familiarize yourself with the stock at your local nurseries. While inventories at big box retailers may change rapidly between visits, smaller local nurseries will often have a consistent list of what they carry. They may even publicize

the list ahead of the growing season. Ask questions during your scouting missions. Maybe the nursery would be willing to bring in a certain species for you or point you in the direction of a better source.

Mail Order

Mail order is another option for sourcing plants. Typically, they ship bareroot (without soil) or in small pots. I've ordered landscape plugs via the mail as well as purchased them directly from nurseries and specialty propagators. There are a few important things to consider when sourcing via the mail.

First, be sure you know from where the plants originate—especially when planting in spring. Speak with the suppliers and get their opinion on when to schedule a shipment so that you have the best chance for success. You may need to plan for a period of hardening off (slowly introducing the plants to the site conditions to avoid shock) when they arrive. Secondly, be sure you know when they will arrive and that someone will be home to receive them. Shipping plants in boxes will subject them to a multitude of temperatures. If the delivery company leaves them on your front steps in the sun, they may be stressed or dead by the time you get home. Thirdly, open the boxes immediately. Using the information you gathered from the distributor, decide whether the plants need to be hardened off. Chances are they have been traveling for a few days and will appreciate some time in a partially shaded area before being transitioned to full sun. Ask your friends and neighbors for recommendations on mail order sources and be sure to read the reviews.

Sometimes you will not be able to find everything on your list. It's helpful to have alternatives in mind that will work as substitutions. If I am being specific about an uncommon variety or cultivar, I will usually include a suitable alternative in the comments section of my plant list. If I am unable to find my first choice, I will make note of this for future projects and move the substitution into the main plant list.

Maintenance Plan

Chapter six will discuss meadow maintenance in detail. However, it's important to mention creating a maintenance plan in this design section as well. You can make your best efforts in site preparation, design, and installation, and the garden can still fail or not live up to its potential because the maintenance of it is misunderstood.

One of the advantages of a meadow is that it can be treated as a plant system or plant community. Generally, you will be able to avoid fussy species-specific maintenance if you choose. I still include details and tricks that I learn during my research in the comments (or maintenance) columns of my plant lists. Should you have the time and energy, these tweaks may prolong bloom time, prevent flopping, encourage or discourage reseeding, or other desirable improvements.

As you will learn in chapter six, a maintenance plan can be arranged by season, be a list of monthly to-dos, or be further dialed-in to break tasks down by week. Maintenance will also vary as the years go on and the meadow becomes more established. For example, year one may emphasize supplemental watering and targeted weeding, while year three may include division of larger perennials or propagation and replacement of biennial species.

Money Matters

One area we have yet to discuss is budget. Costs will vary greatly based on the scope of the project, the area in which you are purchasing materials, and your patience. If you want a mature garden right out of the gate, plan to pay more. I encourage clients to design as if a budget doesn't exist, and then value engineer, scale back, or phase the project to fit within their budget. That way your dreams and designs are not immediately limited by cost considerations, and you can have more fun.

Value engineering might mean that you remove certain rarer species or purchase smaller plants than you had initially planned. Scaling back might apply to the overall scope or just certain elements. Phasing means that you are able to achieve the original goal but over a longer duration. An example would be to plant half the species in the spring and wait to install the second half in the fall. Also keep in mind the cost savings of growing from seed.

The most simplified maintenance practices following the establishment year include a late winter cut back and the removal of organic material to the compost pile, spot watering during extended periods of drought, targeted weeding, deliberate seeding, and monitoring for pests. Taking notes is also important as you become more familiar with the species you have selected and the insects and other wildlife that come to visit your garden.

Design Inspiration

The following paragraphs will build upon the design elements we discussed earlier in the chapter. The previous section provided an introductory understanding of elements such as color, layers, texture, and seasonality. This next section will demonstrate how to apply certain design approaches such as how to lay out structural plants versus seasonal drifts and how to incorporate seeding into the mix. You may choose to focus on one or several of these approaches as you further create your design or strategy.

Grass Swaths + Matrices

Grasses and grass-like plants (sedge and rush species) are a central element in meadows and prairies. Their texture and movement knit together the other showier flowers. With careful observation you will see that they too will have their moments in bloom. There are a couple of simple ways to consider them in your designs.

First, you may choose to create drifts of the same species. Here they will be laid out in odd numbered groupings of undulating organic shapes. Using repetition of these groupings will lead your eye through the design.

Planting loose matrices (or intermixed) groupings of several species of grass will create a hazy naturalized effect into which you can plant

Groups of grasses arranged informally make an ideal foundation for a meadow planting in which to plant your flowering perennials, biennials, and annuals.

your other flowering plants. Instead of distinct single-species drifts, the textures are spread throughout the overall planting. Depending on the scale of your meadow, you may wish to create more than one set of grass matrices with a few different species in each. This will create more complexity and drama. Think of this approach as drifts of different matrices.

Remember that simple is beautiful. You can even create a matrix of just one grass species into which the other flowers will be planted. Examples of grasses for drifts and matrices are included on page 148 in chapter seven.

These coneflower seedheads provide a dramatic silhouette against the frothy little bluestem plants in mid-winter.

These salvia are planted in loose drifts to amplify their seasonal color. After they bloom, they can be cut back to make tidy clumps of new foliage.

Placement of Structural Plants

Structural plants consist of those species with distinctive forms. Usually this is achieved through a height differentiation by placing taller structural species individually amidst shorter plants. Their flower spikes, umbels, or seed heads may tower over their neighbors. They are most effective when placed on their own in a random scattered pattern. There are certain upright grasses that are vertical enough in their overall form to qualify as structural plants. Thick strappy leaves and other distinctive foliage can also be architectural—especially in contrast to the diffuse glow of the surrounding grasses and more delicate textures. Examples of structural plants are included in the dry sun emergent list on page 144 as well as those listed as emergent in the layer category of the other lists.

Drifts of Seasonal Color

Drifts of seasonal color include plants that may be rather non-descript when not in bloom. These species are best placed in odd-numbered swaths so they can really shine together during their week or two in flower. If you have the space, consider repeating these groupings so your eye moves around the garden. When considering which species and how many of each to include, be sure to refer to the bloom times in your plant list.

As flowers are desirable for humans and wildlife alike, you want to be sure to select enough diversity to have continuous blooms through the year. If you don't have the space for that much variety, at least include species that flower in each season. Examples of species good for seasonal drifts in sun are *Dalea purpurea* (purple prairie clover) and *Salvia nemorosa* 'Caradonna' (Caradonna meadow sage). For a part-shade meadow, *Iris cristata* (dwarf crested iris) and *Mertensia virginica* (Virginia bluebells) are good examples because they have showy blooms but then go dormant in the summer. Plants

Include self-seeding annuals, like these lemon beebalm (*Monarda citriodora*), for first-year color in new plantings. Often it will take one to two years for newly establishing perennials to flower with any impact.

that fade or go dormant after they bloom will need to be planted with other species that emerge and fill the gaps but do not out compete them. Ferns are good candidates in this part-shade example.

Annuals for First Year Color

Unless you are purchasing two-gallon (7.5 L) pots of perennials or working with large divisions, it can take one to two years for a new perennial meadow to have a strong impact. Have you ever heard the adage: *sleep, creep, then leap*? As a general rule, perennials focus on putting down roots in the first year, foliar expansion in the second, and begin spreading and flowering heavily in their third. This will vary by species, growing conditions, and initial plant size—especially the size of the root system upon installation.

One way to achieve immediate gratification is to include a selection of annual plants to intermix in the voids during the first, and even second, season. One additional trick to consider is to choose self-seeding annuals. They will fill in the gaps and provide extra spontaneity in years to come.

Be sure to include annuals that emulate those you might find in a meadow or prairie. You can either plan for pockets of annuals that you seed or replace each year, or scatter them throughout the planting. After laying out and installing your perennials, use the design techniques discussed above to help with placement of the annuals. They will be the central color source for the first year. Examples of annual species are included on pages 150–152 in chapter seven.

Groundcover + Living Mulch

As discussed in the layers section, creeping groundcovers and other short plants are an essential component to your new meadow. Not only will they help with moisture retention and weed suppression, but they also perform an underrated role of tying the planting together on the ground plane. They are most visible in spring before the taller plants fill in.

Acting as a green, or living, mulch, these low plants will cover the soil beneath the taller showier plants. They also act as an insurance

or just self-seeding annuals or you may choose to include seed of some of the surrounding species so you have plants of different ages. You may wish to scatter one species at a time in certain areas or create seed mixes. It may be desirable to create a couple of different mixes and place them in different bands or swaths within your new garden. There are endless combinations of species that you could include in your seed mixes. For more information on starting from seed, see pages 100–101 in chapter five.

Moving on from the Planning Stage

By becoming more familiar with your site, you've learned how to create a base plan, determine the rough number of plants you will need, and come up with a planting plan or strategy. With your goals and site assessment guiding you, you've begun to consider how some essential design elements such as colors, textures, and seasonality will impact your design. You know how to source—including the advantages of working with your local nurseries. I've covered design inspiration topics to help you think about and work with various layers including grass swaths, structural plants, annual color, and seed mixes.

You are ready to begin preparing your site for installation. The next chapter will cover how to best remove existing vegetation and whether amendments such as mulch or compost will benefit your project. You will now move from paper and spreadsheets to tools and soil in the final step before planting your new meadow.

policy so that when a taller perennial dies there in another layer below to occupy the space. As with all of the species you select for your project, be sure the groundcovers are not aggressive. Robust species are welcome, but aggressive plants may outcompete their neighbors and dilute your design—becoming a problem in the future. As the taller plants grow and expand, the living mulch will ebb and flow around their bases. Look for plants that will tolerate partial sun conditions. Examples of species that will function well as a living mulch are included in the list on page 158.

Scattering Seed Mixes in the Voids

Another way to close the gaps and create additional spontaneity in your design is to scatter seeds once the larger plant material has been installed. You may isolate specific types of plants to include in the seed layer such as just grasses

4

Preparing the Meadow Site

How to Get Rid of Existing Vegetation and Manage the Soil to Get Ready for Growing

You've chosen the location for your new meadow, created a plant list, and are ready to begin prepping the site. Evaluate what is existing. Is it turf, a patch of weeds, a declining shrub bed, or something else? The existing vegetation will dictate what your options are for your initial site preparation. We will review methods to clear the site of existing vegetation while minimizing labor both in the long and short term. We will also discuss some the drawbacks and benefits to using different types of mulch. Knowing that many people have homeowners' association (HOA) guidelines to consider, different edging techniques for how to make your meadow look deliberate will also be addressed. The first step after identifying what needs to be removed is selecting the best method to do so.

Removing Exiting Vegetation

Most likely, you will need to remove existing vegetation prior to installing your new planting. It is important to disturb the soil and seed bank (dormant seeds in the soil) as little as possible. The amount of disturbance will depend on the type of vegetation and number of plants that need to be removed—and your method of choice. For example, if you are taking out woody species like shrubs or small trees, there will be unavoidable disturbance if you remove the roots. Select the method that effectively removes the vegetation in question, but does so with the least amount of disturbance. Below are some options for getting rid of existing plant material in preparation for your new meadow.

The showy white-to-lavender flowers of clary sage (*Salvia sclarea*) rise 3 to 4 feet (91 to 122 cm) above the surrounding Mexican feathergrass (*Nassella tenuissima*) and seedheads of wild bergamot (*Monarda fistulosa*) in the background and Schubert's allium (*Allium schubertii*) in the foreground.

Eliminating Shrubs + Trees

If there are small trees or shrubs in the area you plan to plant, you will need to start by removing them. Larger established plant material will be labor intensive to take out. One option to consider for less disturbance to the soil is the cut and paint method. This is when you cut the shrub or tree back to a stump and paint the exposed surface with a systemic herbicide. You are then able to leave the roots in the ground and plant around the stumps. This reduces the amount of labor and minimizes disturbance. The choice to use an herbicide as a tool is a personal one that must be weighed cautiously. Trust your own research and ethics as to whether this may be the best approach for your project—and always follow the label.

Sheet mulching, or lasagna gardening, involves layering various organic materials, such as the cardboard and straw shown here, on the site to smother the existing vegetation and build soil.

Sheet Mulching

One of the simplest methods to create a new garden area is to sheet mulch (also known as lasagna gardening). This is best for smaller projects. It involves layering various organic materials in a location to smother the existing vegetation and build the soil. While this technique is less labor intensive than stripping sod, for example, it will require some patience. Organic matter takes time to decompose, so in areas with four seasons, this is best started in late summer or fall, for planting the following spring. The plant species you intend to grow in the space and the quality of the existing soil will inform which layers are best to incorporate in this practice.

First, sheer the existing herbaceous vegetation (sod or groundcover) by string trimming or mowing at the lowest setting. You can leave the clippings in place provided they are not full of undesirable seeds. Next, add additional green compost, including lawn clippings, up to a few inches. Then, cover the area in non-glossy newsprint—several overlapping layers thick. Next, add finished compost and additional green materials if available. Top these layers with corrugated cardboard that is free of tape and staples. Finally, top dress the area in several inches of carbon-rich materials like straw, chopped leaves, pine needles, or wood mulch—avoiding hay and other elements with potential weed seeds.

While it will take time to decompose, there are variations on this recipe that allow you to plant directly into the layers. One of the largest benefits of this method is to utilize materials already on site, such as leaves, compost, and lawn clippings. However, many meadow species don't require nearly the amount of soil amendments that were customary and thought to be beneficial in years past. In fact, *highly amended soils often welcome rapid weed growth more than they benefit new plants.* I've successfully simplified these steps by skipping the carboard and carbon layers, and topdressing with clean topsoil. This allows you to plant young plants while the smothering and decomposition is occurring below. Be aware of your existing soil conditions and the needs of the species you plan to include when deciding which layers to incorporate.

Death to Sod

In some cases, especially for larger areas where other techniques are not practical, a one-time judicious use of systemic herbicide is an approach to consider. In this case, you can plant directly into the dead sod. While this is a heated subject, numerous well-known landscape professionals employ this method as a way to prepare a site. The argument I have most often read in favor of this approach is that because it is a one-time application to convert ecologically devoid turf to a biodiverse garden, the benefits outweigh the concerns. As mentioned above, I encourage you to consider all approaches and decide if this tool is one that makes sense for your project.

Use a hose to lay out the shape of your bed. Paint the outline using marking paint and remove the hose. Using a spade or straightedge shovel, create a clean edge by remove three to four inches (8–10 cm) of soil along the line and toss it into the new planting area. This will help you keep turfgrasses out of the new bed in the future. Once the bed shape and edges are established, spray the turf on a day with little to no wind to prevent drift. Wait until the turf has browned. Consider watering it a couple of times to see if new weed seeds germinate. You may wish to spot spay an additional time if this is the case. Wait an additional couple of weeks and then plant directly into the dead grass.

Plant Through It

Another option to consider is to plant through your existing lawn. I recommend this only when your grass is already weak and patchy. This results in a looser look with changes occurring over time. Be sure to select species that hold their own against turfgrasses. As the plants mature, they will begin to shade out the existing lawn. Avoid this technique with aggressive grasses, including zoysia and Bermuda grass. Cultural practices such

This section of lawn was carefully sprayed with a one-time herbicide treatment to make way for a biodiverse mini-meadow planting.

In this section of designer and author Benjamin Vogt's home landscape, he experimented with planting plugs and over-seeding directly into existing patchy turf.

as cutting back on irrigation will impact the ratio of turfgrass that remains.

In this approach, it is important to kill or remove the turf in the areas to be planted. Be sure to clear an area at least twice the size of the new plant containers. This will further limit competition during the establishment period. Be sure to trim the area to a height of two to three inches (5–8 cm) prior to planting. This will make it easier to monitor your new plants.

Strip the Sod

Depending on the scale of the area being converted, you may wish to remove the existing sod by hand. This can be done mechanically with a flat spade. If it's a larger area, you may wish to rent a sod cutter from a local tool and equipment rental supplier. This will speed up the process, but you will need to factor the cost of rental and transportation into your overall budget. If the sod you are stripping is in good health, consider using it to patch other areas on your property. If not, add it to your compost pile. If the plant palette you have chosen includes heavy feeders, consider retaining as much of the topsoil as possible by knocking it from the roots of the stripped turf. As mentioned, many meadow and prairie species prefer a lean soil. If your plant selection includes more of these, add the nutrient-rich topsoil to the compost for later use in your veggie plots or traditional flower borders.

To Mulch or Not to Mulch

One widely debated topic that often gets brought up in gardening circles and at plant conferences is whether or not to mulch. When it comes to meadow design, my simple answer is no. A more nuanced answer would be that it depends on the site, the local rainfall and irrigation methods, and the plant species that have been selected. Mulch,

For smaller areas, remove the sod by hand with a flat spade and add it to your compost pile, or use it to patch bare spots in other locations in your lawn.

especially wood mulch, is greatly overused in landscape design.

Somewhere during the history of garden design, it was decided plants need to be separated and surrounded by a sea of bark mulch. This is not the aesthetic we are going for when designing meadows. Meadows are dynamic plant systems that interact with each other. It is their overlaps and embraces that set them apart. We use tighter spacing to emulate natural plant communities.

There are a few reasons to use mulch in the first growing year. First, mulch helps to retain moisture. If you live in an area that does not get much rainfall, mulch will help reduce the frequency of supplemental watering during establishment. Second, clean mulch will reduce the germination of weeds. As it is difficult to know if the mulch you are purchasing is entirely free of weed seeds, this is a bit of a gamble. Third, it insulates the soil from frost and extreme temperature fluctuation. Lastly, it may increase biological activity while adding nutrients and organic matter.

As we've discussed, many meadow and prairie species prefer lean soil, so adding organic matter

Gravel Gardening

REDUCED MAINTENANCE BENEFITS:

1. less weeding

2. less irrigation

3. little to no fertilizer

4. little mowing; perhaps once per year

5. treat as a plant system; cut back in late winter or early spring

I began experimenting with gravel gardening around the time that James Hitchmough's *Sowing Beauty* was being published. I was working as a horticulturist for a municipality in the parks department—looking for ways to increase naturalistic perennial planting displays while reducing maintenance for our staff. I had been reading about how many prairie, meadow, and steppe plants preferred lean soils and how amended soils often favored weed growth.

Once planting season was over, the remainder of the summer and fall seasons were mostly spent trying to keep up with the weeds that would proliferate in the display beds that had been so well-intentionally amended over the years. When an opportunity arose for a complete redesign of an existing garden, I submitted a proposal to trial a gravel garden in its place.

I referenced the work of Cassian Schmidt at the Hermannshof Gardens in Germany and Jeff Epping at Olbrich Botanical Gardens in Madison, Wisconsin, as well as research from the Landscape Architecture Department at the University of Sheffield in England. Each had employed a similar approach.

As I was working on an existing greenway that was listed on the National Register of Historic Places, the garden had to be dug into the median versus being built on top of it. As such, we removed roughly five and a half inches (14 cm) of topsoil and existing vegetation. Design guidelines and budget constraints prevented edging the exterior, but I would recommend keeping the gravel contained and separate from surrounding soils when possible.

After laying out the small pots and landscape plugs, the plants were installed directly into the new gravel layer.

Here is the same garden one year later in late summer.

CREATE YOUR OWN GRAVEL GARDEN:

1. Remove five to six inches (13-15 cm) of topsoil or create a five to six inch (13-15 cm) raised bed on top of the soil.

2. Fill with ⅜ inch (1 cm) washed local gravel. Be sure there are no smaller stones or fines in the mix. Do not use limestone as it breaks down over time. Calculate the amount of gravel you will need by multiplying the length and width of the garden by the depth of the gravel. For example, a fifteen- by twenty-foot (4.6 x 6 m) garden with six inches (15 cm) of gravel would require 15 x 20 x .5 = 5.5 cubic yards (4.2 m³). See an online materials calculator to double check your math.

3. Do not use filter fabric or any other barrier between the stones and existing soil.

4. Rake evenly.

5. Lay out plants nine to eighteen inches (23-46 cm) on center using small plants such as plugs and four-inch (10 cm) pots.

6. Plant directly into the gravel. Be careful not to disturb the existing soil below.

7. As you plant, gently shake excess nursery soil off the rootzones into a large bucket.

8. Water generously upon completion.

9. Depending on your climate and the time of year, daily watering for the first few weeks may be necessary as the roots find their way to the subsoil.

10. You may need to briefly water multiple times per day to cool the stone while the plants establish and begin to shade the stone with their foliage.

11. Slowly back off on watering; monitoring daily at first especially during dry spells.

ADDITIONAL TIPS:

1. Select deep-rooted and drought-tolerant plants. See the dry sun lists and groundcover list on pages 140, 142–144, 158–160.

2. Wait until late winter or early spring to cut back previous year's growth to four inches (10 cm). Use a string trimmer or garden shears. A brush mower or other larger equipment may be used, but use caution to avoid disturbing the gravel.

3. By raking or blowing, remove all plant debris from the site and compost. Do not leave organic matter on the gravel as this will encourage weed seed germination.

4. If adding bulbs in the fall to start the bloom season earlier, cut the garden back in late winter prior to the bulbs emerging.

5. Treat the planting as a community. Free yourself from meticulous species-specific maintenance.

6. If certain species do not thrive, select others as replacements.

7. Keep an observation journal for the insects and other wildlife that visit the site.

Here a portion of the planting has been installed through a compost layer that has been added as a top dressing to help retain moisture on this sandy site. More plants were then added to tighten the spacing.

Topdressing with Compost

While it's usually unnecessary and disadvantageous to amend the soil, topdressing with clean, finished compost can be beneficial during the first year. Respecting the no-till method, for an initial boost of nutrients during the establishment period, add a layer of one to two inches (2–5 cm) of compost to the project site prior to planting. Steeply drained and sandy soils will benefit from the introduction of additional organic matter that will help to hold moisture in the soil. If you already have rich loamy topsoil, I would discourage you from adding any compost. If not, a thin layer of compost offers the benefits of mulching that were mentioned above while acting as a slow release fertilizer for the young plants.

More Set Up Considerations

In addition to mulch or compost, there are a few additional aspects to consider. If you live in a particularly dry area or are planting during a dry season, it would be best to water in advance of your installation. You may also wish to clearly define the edges and transitions of your new garden—especially in neighborhoods with HOAs based on traditional landscapes.

Watering Before Planting

If you live in a dry climate with little or infrequent rainfall, you may wish to water the freshly prepared site one to two days prior to planting. You want the soil to be watered slowly and deeply to prevent runoff. You also want to be sure that the site is not flooded or muddy on planting day because, in addition to being messy, walking on or working with soils that are wet will irreversibly damage their structure and compact them. To water deeply and reduce runoff, water for short intervals with periods of time in between for

may be undesirable. Ideally you have selected certain species that will function as living green mulch. In time, as the plants fill in, they will also shade the soil, reducing weed infiltration and helping with moisture retention. The plants and spacing you have chosen will knit together and provide many of the functions of mulch—and they will do so more quickly in the absence of a thick smothering layer of wood mulch.

One of the primary benefits of mulching is to recycle materials on site. So instead of paying for bagged mulch or sending your yard waste to the landfill, consider chopping your leaves with a mulching lawnmower or chipping small branches with a residential chipper. In most cases, the best place for this DIY mulch is in your veggie garden, your more traditional shrub and flower borders, or the compost pile.

infiltration. This will ensure that the subsoil is adequately moist when you plant, and your subsequent watering will be better absorbed. We will discuss post-installation watering in chapter six.

Clean Edges + HOA Considerations

One thing to consider when preparing your site is the importance of clean edges. While this is a personal preference and depends largely on the location of the garden, there are other factors to take into account. The two worth noting here are curb appeal and homeowners' association (HOA) guidelines.

Naturalistic gardens and designed meadows are becoming more widely desired and accepted. However, this transition toward ecological landscaping comes after years of conventional lawn maintenance practices and traditional flower and shrub borders—leaving room for misunderstandings. HOAs may have rules in place that were originally intended to discourage landscape neglect.

One easy way to make sure your garden looks deliberate is to keep the edges clearly defined. This can be as simple as a mowing strip (section of mown turf) between the meadow and the sidewalk or other hardscape. The other option is to edge the garden either with a spade or shovel, or a material such as metal edging, stone, cobble, or brick. While the hand-dug edge is more laborious because it requires more upkeep, it is also more flexible and can be especially effective when converting existing lawn to meadow over time. It allows for garden expansion as the meadow fills in or as you decide to add plants.

In recent years, you may have heard of HOAs challenging homeowners about their landscape choices. Paradigm shifts take time. As we learn more about the impacts of climate change and species loss, we are witnessing a move away from the chemically treated lawn obsession of the past toward a more naturalistic landscape. This expands the definition of a garden or landscape to include habitat, wildlife, and biodiversity. Be sure to review your HOA documents to be sure you are not blatantly violating any of the covenants.

Good Site Preparation Takes Time

You now know how to evaluate and prepare your site for planting. Be sure to plan for ample time to do so—including any lead time necessary based on the individual practices you will incorporate or supplies you need to acquire. Make a step-by-step list of the process and calculate all materials needed. Assign an estimated amount of time that each step will take to help you plan your approach and block off enough time to achieve all that you have set out to accomplish. This will ensure you have enough time to prepare your new garden space for planting.

A mowing strip around the exterior of this grassy meadow planting at Chanticleer Garden provides a clipped contrasting border to the movement and texture of the wilder space within.

5

Planting Your Mini Meadow

Planting Methods, Tools, and Timing for Success

You have now reached the section on acquiring and installing the flowers and grasses. We've covered how to plan and prepare for your new meadow and it's finally time to play with plants. In this chapter you'll discover what size plants to look for and the best planting techniques for each. We'll discuss growing from seed and other ways to stretch your budget. You'll get a better understanding for when to spend a little extra to get what you want.

We'll review best times to plant and best tools to use. You'll learn layout and installation strategies to simplify the guesswork when it comes time to finally start placing your new plants in their new home. Let's begin by exploring how to select plants and what the best sizes will be for your project and budget.

Plant Selection

Plants are available for purchase in all sizes—from packets with tiny seeds that fit in the palm of your hand to balled and burlapped (B&B) trees that require cranes to lift and place. In the case of herbaceous plants, most perennial species are traditionally available in gallon (4 L) or half-gallon (2 L) pots. Annuals are typically sold in four- and six-packs or by the flat. Specialty plants may be sold in three- and four-inch (0.5 L) pots. Some larger grasses may be sold in three- or five-gallon (12–20 L) containers. In recent years landscape plugs have grown in popularity. These are species grown in flats where the emphasis is on establishing deep roots in a compact size. These differ from annual flats of four-packs due to the size and depth of the rootzone.

Goldenrod, mountain mint, and big bluestem combine to create a layered habitat in this seeded meadow at Mount Cuba Center.

Landscape Plugs

Landscape plugs are one of my favorite ways to purchase plants because they allow you to stretch the budget. Essentially, landscape plugs are what the nursery industry purchases and plants up into half- and one-gallon (2–4 L) pots. These larger pots get a head start in the greenhouse, but if you purchase them at the beginning of the season, you will see that you are paying for mostly soil. If you are willing to be patient, landscape plugs planted directly in the landscape will catch up to the larger pots in a matter of months, if not weeks.

Another advantage of working with landscape plugs is that they usually come in larger flats (for example, thirty-two plugs in some cases). This will help you to simplify your design because you will not be purchasing thirty-two of every species that caught your attention. Most likely you will choose your favorites and those you wish to repeat en masse.

Another trick I use because of the value for the money is to plant a couple of plugs per hole. So instead of placing fifty plants, you are planting twenty-five that are twice as large. Consider partnering with a friend or neighbor who is also creating a new garden. You can then split the plants in the flats depending on your needs. Be aware that some of the growers that supply landscape plugs only sell wholesale.

OPPOSITE, TOP Landscape plugs are compact and economical, focused on establishing a healthy rootzone to produce a robust plant once installed. They're easy to layout and install.

BOTTOM You can stretch the budget by including more plant material at smaller sizes that quickly catch up to larger, more expensive plant material.

Selecting the Best Plants

When scouting for potential plant material, start by looking at the overall health of the plants in the nursery. Then evaluate the species you are interested in buying. Scout for pests, yellowing leaves, or otherwise stressed plants. If you notice that most of the plants in a certain species are struggling, ask the staff what is going on and consider sourcing those plants elsewhere.

If you've found a large selection of healthy plants, squint your eyes. Select the largest plants of any given pot size. This comes with practice, but is easy to learn. You'll notice that some of the plants are more robust. Those are the best.

Choose the plants with the fullest foliage. While it may be tempting to choose plants with the most flowers, these flowers are using energy that could be directed to the roots and foliage. Unless your new meadow is being created for an upcoming event like a wedding or garden party, consider removing the buds and blooms before you plant. This will direct the energy of the plant into rootzone establishment. You will get a fuller more established plant in less time and be rewarded in future blooms.

When to Splurge on Larger Plants

You may get more for your money by purchasing a larger plant and dividing it. Another reason you may wish to spend more on a plant is because it's uncommon, or difficult to source, in the trade. Some species are particularly challenging to propagate, resulting in higher prices. Some take a long time to reach flowering age from seed, so you will pay more for a mature plant because of the labor involved and the number of years the plants took up space in the nursery. You will have to weigh your options against your budget, but I would encourage you to leave room to splurge on a favorite or two.

Seedheads, like these common milkweed pods, are not only beautiful, but they also provide seed for growing your own plants.

With patience, planning, and research, you can propagate plants of your own.

Starting from Seed

If you have enough lead time, growing from seeds is one of the least expensive ways to create a new garden. You can grow them outdoors or indoors in flats or direct sow them on the site. Direct sowing is the least time-consuming method, but you may have more success growing in pots and flats.

Cold Stratification

For many native species in temperate climates, a period of cold stratification is necessary. Stratification is the treatment of seeds to mimic the conditions in nature that break dormancy. Cold stratification means the seed needs a period of time below a certain temperature. In nature, this prevents seeds from germinating until after winter has passed. This can be simulated using a refrigerator or, if the timing works, by sowing the seeds outdoors before winter—either in flats, pots, or directly on the ground.

If you do decide to simulate this cold phase in the refrigerator, be sure to research whether the seeds require moist or dry stratification and then store them in an airtight bag or container. Each species will have different requirements, but a quick internet search or chat with the supplier will clarify this. As a general rule, I have seen four to five weeks listed as sufficient time for many species, but be sure to verify this will work for the species you have selected. After cold stratifying, your seeds can remain in cold storage for a long time if you aren't ready to sow them.

Growing in Flats

If you are planning to grow from seed, consider adding a column or two in your plant list in which to record species-specific propagation information. I have had success sowing in flats in the fall and allowing Mother Nature to work her magic over the winter. You can then pot them up to

With simple supplies and a little lead time, you can grow much of the plant material for your project or future expansion.

larger containers after they emerge and care for them in a more controlled environment until they are large enough to be planted in their new site.

Germinating seeds in this way offers you the cost-savings of growing from seed, while retaining the ability to be more precise with your design than directly scattering on the site. As you become more experienced and familiar with the germination requirements of each species, you will find there are ways to be intentional with direct sowing as well.

Preparing the Ground for Seed

While I have recommended choosing plant species that fit the existing growing conditions of your site and not amending your soil, there are exceptions. If you are direct sowing seeds and have fast draining soil with a high sand content, you will need to add organic matter to retain moisture. In keeping with the no-till method to avoid stirring the seedbank, add one to two inches (2–5 cm) of finished local compost on top of the existing soil. Water the area and wait two weeks for weeds to appear. Hand-pull or cut off the new weed seedlings. The area will then be ready to seed.

Direct Sowing

Most seeds prefer temperatures over 55°F (13°C) and will germinate in fourteen to twenty-one days. It's best to avoid sowing in summer, so aim for spring and fall depending on the species and your project timeline. Seed suppliers will help with calculating how much seed you will need based on the size of your project area and number of species you plan to include.

If you've decided to direct sow, one of the easiest ways to disperse seed evenly and help to keep them in place is to mix them with sand. Don't use beach sand as this may have salt that can damage the seeds and soil. Mix one-part seeds to eight-parts sand in a coffee can or other small container. Be sure to mix it well so that the seeds are evenly distributed throughout. Scatter the mixture over the prepared soil or between your newly installed plants. I've heard people explain the scattering technique as similar to how one would toss feed for chickens. Once distributed, compress lightly by carefully walking over the seeds or by pressing down gently with your hands.

If you are seeding a larger area, consider renting or borrowing a lawn roller to be sure the seeds make good contact with the soil. Water in lightly using the mist or shower setting on your hose nozzle. Keep the water pressure low as to not disturb the seeds or cause them to float away. If you are working on a slope, use jute or another biodegradable netting to lay across the area. The netting helps to keep the seeds in place and limit erosion in the event of a heavy rain.

Sourcing Seeds

You may harvest seeds from existing plants, buy packets or bulk seed from a store or online source, or trade seeds with your friends. While seed mixes from reputable suppliers take some of the guesswork out of custom mixes, avoid the meadow-in-a-can type of products that you see at

A custom steppe prairie seed mix, designed by James Hitchmough and available commercially, creates a perennial plant community of 26 species.

Best Time to Plant

While the best plant selection and availability is spring, the best time to plant is when you have time. You can plant anytime you can drive a shovel into the ground. There are some caveats to this, but first start by familiarizing yourself with the last and first frost dates in your area.

Frost Dates

An internet search for the first and last frost dates for your state, province, zip code, or postal code yields quick results. It will give you an average date for the last light freeze and first light freeze in your area. A light freeze is defined as 29°F to 32°F (-1.7°C–0°C), which will kill tender plants.

Monitor the ripening of your seeds and collect them before they open—or scatter them directly in bare patches.

nurseries and big box retailers. These mixes often rely on fast-blooming annuals that are short-lived and are easily out competed by aggressive weeds.

If you've selected perennial seeds, one effective way to limit weed infiltration is to mow the area to six inches (15 cm) every six weeks or so for the first growing season. This will prevent most weeds from going to seed while the desirable perennial species you selected have a chance to establish strong roots. If you have also planted larger plants or are growing an annual meadow, do not mow during the growing season. Plan to cut weeds to the ground periodically to limit seed production as well as limiting soil and seed bank disturbance. See more on meadow maintenance in chapter six.

Note that there is still a thirty percent chance of frost occurring before or after these dates. While you can plant outside of this window, it provides a baseline understanding for the growing season in your area.

Rainy Season

Another aspect to consider is when the natural rainy season occurs in your area. Any assistance by Mother Nature to water during plant establishment will mean less labor on your part. Avoid walking in or working the soil when it is wet and muddy to limit compaction. If you have irrigation set up, you can plant anytime during the growing season. We will discuss this in more detail in the next chapter.

Know Your Plant Sources

When purchasing plant material, be sure you know from where it was sourced—especially when working close to frost dates. If the plants have been shipped in from somewhere warmer, you may have to harden them off first to avoid shocking them. Hardening off is a process by which you slowly acclimate a plant to the local climate. This can be applicable to mail order plants, plants that nurseries have brought in from warmer climates, and any seedlings you may have started indoors or in a protected cold frame or greenhouse.

Generally, this process involves placing the plants in a protected area outside during the day and bringing them inside at night for a period of seven to fourteen days. Be sure to slowly acclimate them to full sun over a period of days or you run the risk of burning the foliage. Even if your plants have been in a sunny south-facing window, they will need to be protected from full mid-day sun for a period of time.

In addition to being mindful about the last frost in spring, be sure to also work back from the first frost date in autumn. Some plants, especially grasses or young plugs, require an establishment period prior to dormancy. In my experience young grasses do not overwinter well when installed close to the first frost date. Give them at least four to six weeks of lead time to acclimate. This is also true of most landscape plugs. In the case of plugs, they will often get pushed out of the soil by frost heaves if they have not had adequate time to root-in. Installation schedules depend on a variety of factors. These recommendations are to set you up for the fewest losses.

Planting Methods

We've covered different plant sizes in the plant availability section. Each requires slightly different planting methods with their scale determining the necessary tools. Because I have recommended as little soil disturbance as possible, you will most likely not be installing plants into freshly tilled earth. Therefore, you will need sharp tools appropriate for the size of plants you will be planting.

How to Plant

Dig a hole slightly wider, but no deeper, than the rootzone of the plant you are installing. The soil level of the new plant should align with, or be slightly higher than, the existing soil. This is especially true if you are planning to add any mulch in the first growing season. Avoid piling any soil on top of the crown of the new plant or against the stem.

Also note that many potted plants that you will buy will either have immature roots compared to the size of the pot or will be rootbound and have roots circling the root ball. To check for this, place your hand over the top of the pot and carefully allow the plant to rest between your fingers. Then tip the pot over so the weight of the soil is against your palm. Tap the bottom of the pot lightly and,

ABOVE Tilt the pot with one hand and, with the other, cradle the top of the soil and base of the plant to avoid damaging the root ball.

RIGHT For rootbound plants, gently tease the roots apart before installing. More extensive cases may require a knife.

pot lightly and, using the drainage hole, lift the plastic pot off the root ball. Ideally you should see small white roots holding the soil together. Using your free hand, cup the bottom of the root ball and gently set it into the hole you've prepared. (If the plant is rootbound, set it aside and see instructions below as to what to do.) Fill the rest of the hole with existing soil and press down softly with your hands. Remember to align the top of the root ball with the existing soil level or a little above. Once everything is planted, water the area thoroughly.

Rootbound Plants

Sometimes, especially later in the growing season, the plants you purchase will be rootbound. This means that instead of the roots growing out and down as they would if they were unencumbered, they hit the edge of the pot and began to circle. While this is more problematic in woody plants like trees and shrubs where the circling roots can girdle the trunk, it is still undesirable in herbaceous plants. You will have noticed this after removing the pot per the earlier instructions.

Instead of planting a rootbound plant directly, set it down on the soil to further assess it. If you are not planning to divide the plant, lean it on its side and cut a shallow "x" in the bottom of the root ball. For a perennial in a one-gallon (4 L) pot, use a serrated knife, small handsaw, or Hori Hori (soil knife) to cut an "x" one to two inches (2–5 cm) deep. Next, where the "x" on the bottom meets the edges of the root ball, cut four lines up the sides to the top of the soil. Lightly tease these cuts open. Then place the plant in its new hole and finish planting.

These cuts prune the roots, ensuring that they will not continue to encircle in the root ball and will instead begin to grow outward and downward into the new soil. If the plant is significantly rootbound, you may also wish to lightly trim the aboveground section of the plant to balance the pruning done above and below the soil line. While herbaceous plants that are rootbound will recover quickly using this method, you are sacrificing

Bareroot plants can be tender and must be handled delicately. Be sure to locate the base of the plant and top of the rootzone to align it properly in its new home.

some of the roots. If you find that many of the plants you purchased are rootbound, call the nursery to let them know and consider shopping elsewhere in the future.

Bareroot Perennials

If you have opted for mail order, some plants may ship bareroot (without soil). Typically shipped dormant, these need to be planted when they arrive or potted up in containers until you are ready for them to be installed. Be careful not to let the roots dry out. Immediately upon arrival, soak the rootzone in water for ten to twenty minutes before planting. Whether planting in the ground or in a pot, look at the length of the roots to decide the depth of the hole or size of the pot.

If planting directly, create a hole no deeper than the length of the roots. In the hole, pile a small mound of soil in the center. Feather the roots apart and drape them over the mound. Do the same if planting in a container. Use the soil mound to spread the roots out in different directions. It is important not to install the bareroot plant too deeply. Identify where the crown (aboveground shoots) and the roots meet. This intersection is where the soil level should be after planting or slightly below.

Tools

While there are a multitude of tool options available, I'd like to highlight a few favorites. In addition to a trusty shovel, smaller hand tools will also make your job easier—especially for smaller gardens. Below are a few favorites to consider.

Shovels

Shovels come in many shapes and sizes and are best for larger plant material such as one-gallon (4 L) pots and larger. If you have a trusty shovel on hand, there is no need to go out to purchase anything special. If, on the other hand, this is one of your first garden projects, let this be an excuse to splurge on some quality tools of your choosing.

There are a few types worth listing here. My go-to is a straight shovel. I like flat shovels because they are multipurpose. They can be used to install plants as well as edge a bed. I also prefer short wooden-handled shovels. When choosing yours, try them out and select the one that feels best for you. A long-handled shovel has more leverage for compact soil or stump and rock removal. The trade-off is the added weight and the extra length that can be more cumbersome to maneuver.

Two other shovel types are the spade and sharp shooter. A spade is rounded with a point. The concave shape makes it better for scooping soil. A sharp shooter has a long narrow blade and rounded tip. These work well in tight spaces and also work for digging deep narrow holes for bulb planting. Visit your local hardware store or garden center to see what they have available and what feels best for you.

Trowels + Soil Knives + CobraHeads

For smaller plant material, you'll want to use a trowel (hand shovel) or one of the other smaller hand tools mentioned in this section. These are compact and portable. With tools, the phrase "you

OPPOSITE LEFT Find your-self a proper spade that is comfortable for your size and appropriate for the projects you plan to complete.

OPPOSITE RIGHT From left to right: a rounded spade, flat spade, pitchfork, loppers, adjustable metal rake, watering-wand

RIGHT Clockwise, from top left: gloves, trowel, Felco pruners, mini-snips/shears, floral scissors, folding saw, soil knife

get what you pay for" is definitely true. You will regret buying the least expensive trowel—as it will most likely bend, rust, and be uncomfortable to use. Be sure to pay a little extra for one made from quality materials—with a comfortable handle and sturdy blade.

I typically use a Japanese soil knife (also called a Hori Hori) instead of a trowel. These sharp six-to-seven-inch (15–18 cm) blades are versatile. They are serrated on one side and can be used for digging, dividing, transplanting, and sawing roots. Some even include measurements on them so you can dig the correct hole depth—which is useful when planting bulbs.

The final small tool I use for installing plants is a CobraHead weeder and cultivator. This tool has a long hook with a flat cobra-shaped head on the end. While it can be used for targeted weeding and cultivating, it also works well to plant small plant material such as landscape plugs or small seedlings.

Hand Pruners

While one might not think of hand pruners as a tool for planting, I recommend having them on you at all times in the garden. When you install your new plants, you will want to trim off all flowers and buds as well as any yellow or damaged leaves. In my experience, Felco pruners are worth the investment over less expensive brands. I also have leather holsters that I wear so I can keep track of my pruners and have them nearby—one just for the Felcos and another that fits both the hand pruners and a soil knife.

At a minimum, when I venture out to the garden, I usually have a flat shovel in my hand and my soil knife and Felcos on my hip. These three tools are enough to accomplish many tasks. You will need other task-specific tools for maintenance, which we will cover more in the next chapter.

Planting Layout + Installation Strategies

Similar to the design inspiration ideas discussed on pages 81–84 in chapter three, the following section will give you practical examples of how to strategize your approach to laying out and installing your design. This will help you confidently integrate your plant list, planting design, and actual plants from the theory and research stage to the layout in the field. We will cover the general types of plants (grasses, perennials, annuals, and bulbs) and layers (emergent, mid-, low, and groundcover) and how to use these designations to simplify your installation.

Grasses in winter provide a cloud of texture around the silhouettes of seedheads.

Grass Matrices

Most definitions of meadow include the word grass as an essential component. Ratios of forbs (flowering plants) to grasses vary. Flower-forward plantings are dramatic, while grass-forward plantings are more subtle. The plant lists you created in chapter four will inform these ratios. In this planting method, the grasses are laid out first. You can use one species in drifts or a few

species interplanted with one another. Either way, laying out one species at a time is the easiest way to organize your installation.

At this point you have already determined how many plants will fit in your space and how many of each species you would like to use. Your plant list will also show you the rough height and widths to help you with spacing. Fortunately, meadows are more forgiving than formal designs. There is no ruler or grid in nature, but there are patterns.

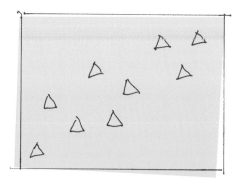

PHASE 1
Laying out drifts of grasses by height

Overlapping drifts of grasses as a first layout element help to organize the planting. If you are using various heights of grasses, place the tallest ones first. You may choose to scatter these throughout the design or group them in certain areas—concentrating them toward the interior or the back if it's along a border. Next, place the medium-height species. These will anchor the design.

A matrix of Mexican feathergrass envelops the lavender and other flowers in this Mediterranean planting.

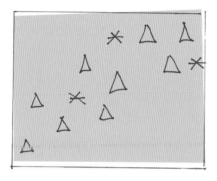

PHASE 2
Spacing by eye or by measurement

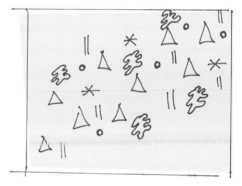

PHASE 3
Planting forbs into the grasses

Approximating the desired spacing, I typically lay out by eye. You may wish to cut a few sticks at various lengths to use as reference, such as twenty-four, eighteen, and twelve inches (60, 46, and 30 cm). I place most plants one to one-and-a-half feet (30–45 cm) on center. Once you have these laid out, step back, assess, and adjust as you see fit.

Into these drifts, you will place your flowering plants. You may wish to plant the medium and tall grasses prior to laying out more plants. Depending on the scale of your planting and whether you have assistance, it may be easier to plant in phases.

Now, select the tallest forb species that you have included. For this example, we will be creating a spontaneous design. The tallest plants will rise above the others, emerging from the grass layers below. Scatter these plants throughout the design. As with the tall grass layer, place them one species at a time, keeping them set back from the edges of the space.

Continue to work your way down by height using the information you've included in your plant list. For plants that are thin or delicate, or for those to which you wish to give more emphasis, place them in odd-numbered groups or drifts. Once you lay out all the medium and tall flowering plants, step back and assess the spacing. Nudge and rearrange prior to installing this next phase.

PHASE 4
Placing the groundcover layer

The final layer are the short plants along the edges and the groundcover plants between the taller ones. I generally think of plants below twelve inches (30 cm), especially those with a spreading habit, to be part of this final layer. These will be spaced six, nine, or twelve inches (15, 23, and 30 cm) on center. While these plants may not stand out as prominently as the taller, more statuesque members, they perform the important role of creating a green or living mulch. As your garden layers knit together over time, you will spend more time enjoying your new space and less time weeding.

The grass matrix approach can be applied all the way down to the groundcover layer with shorter species.

OPPOSITE PAGE After laying out the grasses, artfully place the perennials into the mix, starting with the tallest species and working your way down.

TOP Grass matrices provide drama as they catch the winter light and showcase the various seedheads of flowering perennials.

Perennials + Annuals

Many mini meadows are created using a mixture of perennial flowering plants and grasses combined with annual plants to fill in empty spots, particularly during the first few growing seasons. This planting plan covers how to lay out a garden that combines perennials and annuals together to create a pleasing and natural blend of plants.

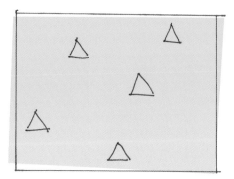

PHASE 1

Lay out the tallest perennial plants

PHASE 2

Place the mid-height perennial plants

If you've decided to include perennials and annuals in your design, be sure to lay out the perennial plants first. While most perennials will tolerate being transplanted if spacing needs to be adjusted in the future, it would be best to have a well-considered layout prior to installation. I include the actual height and width dimensions in my plant list, as well as a column for approximate dimensions. This allows me to group plants by intervals. For example, if I have a species that is twenty-two inches (56 cm) wide and one that is twenty-six inches (66 cm) wide, I will group them in the twenty-four inch (60 cm) category. While I don't worry too much about exact spacing, I'll know to place these plants roughly two feet (60 cm) on center. This helps to speed up lay out and installation, as well as reinforce a look of spontaneity.

Familiarize yourself with the heights and widths of each species on your plant list. You want the plants to fill in and intertwine, but there is no sense in placing them in such a way that they outcompete one another. Place the tallest species first.

Once you have placed the taller perennials, lay the mid-sized selections out on your site using the descending height approach. Sort your plants and place them one species at a time, referring to your list to keep the heights well organized. Follow this with your groundcover layer. Your planting strategy or planting plan will help to inform your layout.

PHASE 3

Planting annuals in pockets or interspersed through the planting

It is important to decide if you want to leave pockets for annuals (see sketches 3a and 3b) or intersperse them throughout (see sketches 4a and 4b). If you've decided to leave pockets, use marking paint to draw out the areas you are reserving for them. If you've decided to intersperse them, wait until the perennials have been placed or installed. The heights and widths you have included in your plant list are based on mature size. As such, there will be space

3A

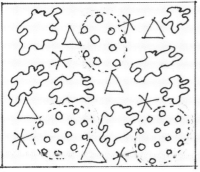

3B

4A

4B

between the perennials in the first growing season for the annuals.

Once the perennial layer has been installed, sort your annuals list by height and repeat the process. With annuals you can really let loose. Imagine you're scattering a seed mix. What whimsy can you emulate with your placement? I still encourage you to place one species at a time in descending order by height.

I will sometimes eyeball where I think certain plants will go and then gently toss them toward that spot and see where they land. If they roll too close to another, I may nudge them slightly—or I may just plant them where they land. Many annuals will bloom all season. Consider how you want the colors and forms to interact. Do you wish to concentrate certain species in drifts? Do you want to group certain species with similar heights? Maybe you want the loud accent colors to be scattered randomly throughout

BELOW Riotous annuals, such as these orange tassel flowers and magenta *Gomphrena*, intermingle with bright salmon perennial flowers of *Agastache* in this first-season mix.

When to edit

One of the things I love about meadow designs are periods of subtlety. Depending on your choices, there will be moments of riotous color and then quieter phases. While I appreciate the excitement that the annual layer offers in the first season, the highly saturated colors and long bloom times can become a bit static. Certain plants and colors will dominate. You may find that you wish to edit, either by pruning and entirely removing certain plants or species, as the season goes on. Trust your instinct and edit slowly. Remember to save seeds of your favorites—either to broadcast directly or save to germinate next year. See pages 150–151 in chapter seven for a list of annuals suggestions that may work well in your meadow.

OPPOSITE Foxglove is a self-seeder that can be scattered or removed as necessary to keep the composition harmonious.

BELOW Tall verbena is a lovely annual perfect for many meadow designs. However, it will self-seed prolifically in certain conditions and may need to be thoughtfully edited.

Bulbs

Bulbs are a wonderful way to extend the bloom time. Many gardeners who live in temperate climates are excited for spring long before it actually arrives. Spring bulbs get the season started early as the other perennials are breaking dormancy and beginning to turn green. Most spring bulbs are planted in the fall and must undergo a cool season in dormancy before they put on their show. Focus on your perennial and annual design for year one, but be thinking of what colors or shapes you may wish to add for year two. By the summer, be ready to explore reputable bulb catalogues to create an order for delivery later in the fall.

Tulips and daffodils are quintessential spring bulbs. Within these species, there is a huge diversity of varieties that bloom at different times of early, mid-, and late spring. Decide which species appeal to you and then choose a few varieties to bloom sequentially. You can also create custom mixes that will bloom simultaneously.

'Spring Green' tulips (*Tulipa* 'Spring Green') and 'Paul Scherer' tulips (*Tulipa* 'Paul Scherer') underplanted with grape hyacinth (*Muscari paradoxum*) and 'Valerie Finnis' grape hyacinth (*Muscari armeniacum* 'Valerie Finnis') in a matrix of autumn moor grass (*Sesleria autumnalis*).

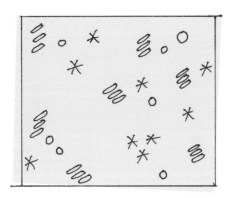

PHASE 1

Lay out taller bulb species before planting

In fall, place taller spring bulbs throughout the planting site, being mindful to organize them according to height. Mix them among existing grasses and perennials, scattering them loosely.

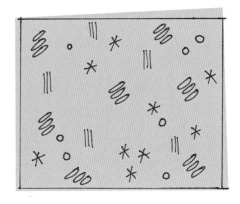

PHASE 2

Mix in mid-height selections

Place mid-height spring-blooming bulbs throughout the garden next, in groups of odd numbers.

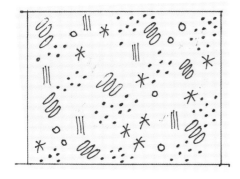

PHASE 3

Add groupings of smaller bulbs

Position and plant scattered groups of smaller bulbs to naturalize throughout the planting.

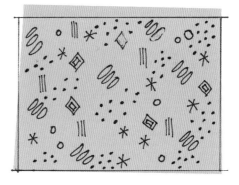

PHASE 4

Layer in a few summer accent bulbs

In spring, add a handful of summer-blooming bulb species to add further layers of texture and color to the planting.

Planning for foliage dieback

There are a few additional notes to consider as you plan for the bulb layer. Most spring bulbs are ephemeral (lasting a short time) and their foliage needs to dieback slowly to send the energy back to the bulb for the following year. If you cut it back, or braid it down, as was common practice in years past, you will deplete the bulb by reducing photosynthesis time. This mildly unsightly period only lasts a couple of weeks. Overall, I have found that distributing bulbs throughout the design verses concentrating them in certain areas is most effective at disguising this.

Accommodating short-lived bulbs

The other thing to keep in mind is that certain bulbs are short-lived. Many tulip varieties for example bloom best their first year and then dwindle over subsequent years. You also have the option of treating some as annuals—cutting them to the ground after they flower and planting new ones in the fall. I recommend researching long-lived options, such as species tulips versus hybrids, for the effort and investment—but the important thing to understand is that certain varieties will only bloom dependably for one to two years.

Bulbs for summer and fall

Bulbs are not just for spring. There are many bulbs to include for summer as well. Summer-blooming bulbs are planted in spring.

Some will overwinter in the proper climates, while others will need to be dug up and stored in a protected area for the winter. For those that need to be protected over winter, wait until the foliage is killed by the first hard frost and then gently lift the bulb from the soil. Mark the location with a small flag or other indicator so you know where to dig.

Be sure to research species-specific storage practices. See pages 161–164 in chapter seven for a list of recommended bulbs species for spring and summer.

The Fluidity of the Design + Installation Process

Understanding how to select and install plants are key skills when designing a new garden. Tips for growing from seed and other budget hacks will help you plan, design, and schedule your project. In addition to your plant lists and planting plan, learning a few layout and installation strategies will give you opportunity to refine your design in the field. The design process is fluid and iterative. It can be simple linear steps forward toward the end goal—or be something more circular where you are improving upon your approach as you gain a more holistic understanding of all of the components.

Hopefully at this point you feel confident to glean elements of all you have learned so far and customize them for your own use. If you have been working on your project as you have been reading, you are now ready to go shopping and make your meadow dreams a reality. If you have been waiting to get the full picture before starting, you are now ready to outline your own process and begin.

Remember to have fun. Relax and experiment. Record the birds, pollinators, and other wildlife that come to visit. I assure you the results will bring you much joy. But remember, proper maintenance is part of the design process and essential to the overall success of your project—especially during the first couple of years while your new meadow becomes established. The next chapter will introduce you to what to expect and how to achieve the best results with the least amount of effort.

Sky-blue star-shaped flowers circle these 1-inch (2.5 cm) blue globe onions (*Allium caeruleum*) emerge from a swath of golden Alexander (*Zizia aurea*).

6

Meadow Maintenance

How to Water, Mow, Weed, and Care for Your Micro Prairie

You've designed and installed your mini meadow in the perfect location. Now you're sitting back sipping lemonade watching your new garden to fill in. If you created a maintenance plan as suggested in chapter three, now is the time to revisit it. If you haven't, now is the time to create one. The most important task immediately following installation is to be sure your plants are getting adequate water.

In addition to enjoyment, watering and weeding will be your primary tasks during the first year. However, in order to know what to weed, you'll need to define the term for yourself and begin to learn to identify the plants that appear in your plot. Don't worry. Over time you will become familiar with what shows up. Even if you don't know how to spell the names in Latin, you will start to identify the plants that are undesirable and how to best manage them.

The species you've decided to include and the size of the plants, or seedlings, will determine if mowing during the growing season is an appropriate practice for your new meadow. We will discuss the importance of leaving the planting standing over winter for year-round interest and habitat. In doing this, you will start the new year with a thorough cut back—either in late winter or early spring.

While there are advantages to knowing the specific maintenance needs of each species, the real advantage is the ability to treat the entire meadow as a plant system. This simplifies your tasks and takes the pressure off expecting to keep a perfectly manicured garden. In fact, it is in the untidiness that you invite the wilderness in and permit yourself the freedom to enjoy your creation. Remember, one of the benefits of a meadow garden is the reduction of maintenance over other styles of gardening.

The grasses, from the pink-mauve of the little bluestem to golden-tan of the blue grama and prairie junegrass, glow in mid-fall light (contrasted by the bold powder-blue foliage of the sea kale [*Crambe maritima*]).

Watering

If you've planted during the rainy season and Mother Nature is taking care of this task—lucky you! If you've planted outside of this window, or live in a drier climate with less rain, you will need to water intermittently during establishment. Having now lived in a home that depends on rainwater and a cistern, I have become extra aware of how precious this resource is. You want your plants to have the moisture they need to thrive, but you also want them to develop deep roots so they can survive on their own as they do in the wild. The best way to encourage this is to water deeply but infrequently.

When to Water

Identify which plants show drought stress first. Typically, there will be a species that will be a good indicator of when your garden needs water. Often this is a plant with large leaves that will droop during the heat of the day. This is called flagging. Flagging indicates a tipping point between health and damage.

Plants release water through pores in their leaves during a process called transpiration. When a plant does not have adequate moisture, or on particularly hot sunny days, the leaves will wilt. By doing this, the surface area exposed to the sun is reduced. When you see this, you know it is time to water.

While it is tempting to want to water your new garden every day, this will not encourage deep roots and resilient plants. The plants will come to expect this and it will require extra effort on your part to attend to them. One of the reasons designed meadows and prairies fit the ecological landscaping model is because they require few inputs (such as water, pesticides, and fertilizers). By waiting until the plants begin to flag before watering, and by watering deeply when you do, you are encouraging the plants to send down deep roots. This way they will be better able to withstand periods of drought in the future.

When you are supplemental watering during plant establishment, eventually you will slowly taper the number of times you water per week. For example, for the first two weeks you may water every three days. Then for the third and fourth week, you will water every five days. By weeks five and six, you will be watering once per week. Eventually, if you have selected species appropriate for your region and the site, you will only water during extended dry periods to keep your meadow looking its best.

How you water also matters. When feasible, commit to only watering in the early morning. This way you will lose less water to evaporation and the foliage will have time to dry out during the day. If you will be watering by hand, decide if you will be using a watering can or a watering wand on a hose. Depending on the length you need, I find it easier to purchase two shorter hoses and attach them versus one long hose.

How Much to Water

If you are using an automated system like sprinklers or a soaker hose on a timer, you will need to determine how long to run it. Set out a rain gauge or clear , shallow container. Time how long

Invest is a quality non-kink hose and watering wand or adjustable nozzle.

LEFT Use a rain gauge to track your automated irrigation and/or the local rainfall. RIGHT If rotating automated sprinklers are already installed on your property, use them in the mornings during establishment and then slowly back off on supplemental waterings aside from extended periods of drought.

it takes to fill it to one inch (2.5 cm). Target to water roughly one to two inches (2.5–5 cm) per week during the establishment period. Drip irrigation or soaker hoses are slightly more difficult to measure. Use a soil knife or trowel to dig a hole and check the moisture of the soil to determine if your garden is getting watered deeply enough. Allow the soil surface to dry out between waterings.

Your soil type will also influence the duration and frequency of watering. If your soil is sandy and sharply drained, you will need to water more often. If it is high in organic matter, which will help to retain water, you will not have to water as much. Use the plant flagging method to determine the sweet spot for your site. If you have designed your meadow in containers, be sure to water all the way through until you see water seeping from the drainage holes.

Watering Frequency for New Seeds + Seedlings

If you have decided to grow plants from seed, you will need to water more frequently to keep the surface layer damp during germination. Young plants have tiny root systems and are more susceptible to drying out faster than larger plants. After scattering, water gently to avoid flooding and disturbing the seeds. Water with a low pressure and pause to give it time to percolate.

Depending on the weather and soil type, you may need to water twice a day at first. Continue watering frequently until your seedlings are four to six inches (10–15 cm) tall. Then begin to taper back the watering schedule to encourage deep roots. If you have installed both seeds and small plants, be sure you are attending to both of their watering needs—keeping the soil surface adequately damp for germination, while periodically watering deeply for the larger plant material.

Pay extra attention during the warmest and driest months. Even an established garden may need periodic supplemental watering to look its best. If you notice the leaves are wilting but the soil is moist, this may indicate that something else is going on such as a pest. Familiarize yourself with common garden pests in your area so you know what to look for.

Adding see-through height and spontaneity, annual tall verbena (*Verbena bonariensis*) makes a welcome self-seeding addition to any meadow planting.

The Gift of Volunteer Plants

Initially, after installing your garden, there will be gaps between the plants. It takes a few seasons for plants to get established. You may also lose some. With a dense meadow planting, I plan for about a ten percent loss over the first couple of years.

Even when you have done your best to select the right species for the space, there will be certain plants that don't make it. That's okay! The plants that do make it will begin to expand. Generally, in smaller gardens, unless one of the goals is erosion control, I avoid species that spread rapidly by rhizomes (horizontal underground stems, that produce shoots and roots). Plants that clump tend to play best with others in these tighter settings.

Have you heard the phrase *nature abhors a vacuum*? As it applies to gardening, it means that unless the conditions are truly unfavorable, plants will fill in bare ground. Slowly, any bare patch of earth will welcome new plants. Those species that love the growing conditions will begin to spread. I welcome these new volunteer plants as they fill in the open spaces. These unplanned moments further create a spontaneity and whimsy that can be difficult to perfect in a planned space.

Learning How to Identify New Plants

It is important to learn what plants look like when they are young seedlings. This takes patience and observation. It can be tempting to treat all unidentified plants as weeds. Pay attention to what grows around what you have planted. Start a list of problem species that are undesirable and learn to identify and remove them when they are young. If you are unsure of what something is, let it remain until you know.

Monitor the area to see if the unknown plants are occurring sporadically or en masse. If you decide the new volunteers are welcome additions, you may still wish to cull some of the more enthu-siastic species and allow only certain individuals to remain in strategic places. Watch how the parent plants perform in the space to know what to expect as these seedlings mature.

Another joy in a new garden is when plants arrive that you didn't include—species outside of the initial plant palette. Maybe they were in the seed bank in the ground waiting for the right time to germinate or maybe they blew in and found a home amongst their new friends. Be patient with the seedlings that grow. Give them time to reveal themselves to you and edit judiciously.

Monitor for aesthetic balance. Are their certain species that are becoming too robust and overwhelming the composition? Also look out for species that take longer to establish and be sure they are not crowded out before they have a chance to stake their claim. Editing is an ongo-ing creative process that is key to the long-term success of your design.

Consider how many plants can occur in a small space in a meadow. There can be as many as twenty to thirty species in one square yard (0.8 m²). Volunteer plants are a gift that help you

Allowing volunteer plants, like this amaranth and euphorbia, to pop up where they may and editing judiciously creates unexpected whimsy that can otherwise be difficult to achieve in a designed planting.

fill in space by choosing their own placement and showing you what preforms best in your conditions.

Certain plants will do better than others from year to year. The layered density and diversity that occurs over time creates resilient communities that thrive during challenging annual changes, such as a prolonged drought or an unusually wet spring. Keep this in mind as you edit seedlings in the spring and spread seeds in autumn.

What Is a Weed?

The second most important task after watering is weeding. First, decide how you wish to define a weed. I like the definition that *a weed is a plant in the wrong place*. This leaves it up to the viewer, or gardener in our case, to determine what constitutes a weed.

There are legal definitions such as those included on Federal and State Noxious Weed lists in the United States. Depending on where in the world you live, there may be a list of species that are detrimental to agriculture or livestock and must be managed on your property. As we are discussing small-scale residential meadow design, I just want to bring your attention to the fact that these lists exist. They may be a good starting point for you to determine what to look out for as you begin to learn to identify young plants in your garden.

Once you have begun to determine which plants are problematic or unwelcome, find ways to limit their spread. As I have emphasized elsewhere, one of the most important aspects to minimizing maintenance is to limit the disturbance to the soil seedbank. The more you turn the soil unnecessarily, the more weeds seeds will be brought to the surface. Depending on how you approach it, even the act of weeding itself can create more weeds.

Hand Pulling

One of the best times to hand-pull weeds is the day after it rains or after watering. Be sure the garden has had adequate time to dry out so that you are not working in mud and compacting the soil. While there is still space to do so, you may also want to use a kneeling pad, or board, to distribute your weight. Only hand-pull small seedlings. Pull from the base of the plant to avoid breaking the stem. You can even hold the soil in place with the other hand as you pull.

Once the seedlings begin to mature, you will be pulling up larger rootzones and disturbing the soil. As tempting as it may be to go through and pull larger weeds, you will be making more work for yourself in the long run.

Cutting to Avoid Soil Disturbance

Once undesirable plants are of a decent size, you will want to remove them by cutting them down. You can use hand pruners, scissors, or lawn sheers. Cut them right at the ground level. You want to starve the roots by removing the aboveground section of the plant to prevent it from photosynthesizing. Rather than chase the same weeds every day, give them time to get some height on them and then go for it! Just be sure the plants are not close to going to seed and are not shading out the plants you've intentionally included.

While this technique is effective much of the time, you may run into species that return over and over. Determine which species these are so

that you can identify them early. In the case of problematic weeds that continue to resprout, you will have to carefully remove the root.

Tap-rooted plants such as dandelions come out fairly easily with a short-handled dandelion weeder or a soil knife. Using either, insert the tool straight down close to the base of the leaves as deep as you can. Then tilt the tool slightly as you grip the top of the plant. You may hear a popping sound as the taproot breaks. Provided you remove enough of the rootzone, the plant should not reappear.

What to Do with Weeds that Continue to Return

Certain species can be extremely difficult to eradicate. Plants that spread by rhizomes or stolons (aboveground runners) will often resprout from any remaining roots or shoot fragments left in the soil. This means that each time you attempt to remove them, you may be creating more—while also disturbing the seedbank. I can think of several species that are particularly challenging like this in the areas I have lived and gardened.

When you come up against an invasive or highly aggressive species, you may want to explore other tools in your toolbox. Check with your local government or university-based agricultural agency or native plant society for resources on how to manage invasive species in your area. Often there are species-specific fact sheets on best management practices.

A judicious herbicide application may be suggested in certain instances. Working within a tightly planted garden such as a meadow, you will need to be extra cautious in its application as to not injure any of the surrounding plants. You can paint it directly on the weeds or use a spray bottle with a directed nozzle. Be sure to apply it on a sunny day with little to no breeze—and always follow the instructions on the label.

A lawnmower set at its highest setting can be used to keep unwanted fast-growing weeds from going to seed while desirable species establish.

LEFT Some hard-to-kill weeds like this Canada thistle may require chemical intervention to eradicate.

While there are organic formulations and other alternatives to synthetic herbicides, if you'd prefer to avoid harsh chemicals you will need to exhaust the plant by other means. Staying in front of seed production is key to weed management. Beyond that, be consistent in cutting the tops of the weeds down to the ground periodically.

If you are tempted to delicately follow the roots and try to remove the entire plant or patch of plants, do so once—so you're disturbing the seedbank as few times as possible. Precise tools such as a Hori Hori knife or other hand weeder are preferable to large hoes or other cultivators. Hoes and cultivator tools are best for the veggie patch or other highly managed areas.

Mowing to Reduce Weeds

Mowing is another tool for weed management and overall meadow maintenance. For weed management, mowing can be implemented during the first and possibly second growing seasons. If you are growing your meadow from seed or a combination of seed and small plants, you can mow every six weeks or so to six inches (15 cm) during the first year. This prevents the majority of weeds from going to seed. It also keeps the crowns of the developing grasses and perennials in full sun as they continue to establish strong roots.

The trade-off is that you will be sacrificing flowers during this time. It will not work if you have included annuals or more mature perennials in your design. This method is most effective in reducing maintenance in larger spaces.

You may wish to carry this into the first few months of the second growing year. Eventually you will want to back off so that your plants will be able to grow tall and have a chance to flower. It's a balance of patience and simplifying maintenance. If you'd prefer to have your meadow blooming in its first year, periodic mowing during the growing season will not work for you.

As we've discussed, a huge advantage of naturalistic and ecological landscape design is to think of the plantings as communities. As such, you can simplify the maintenance practices and treat them as a whole versus worrying as much about species-specific maintenance as in traditional perennial horticulture.

Create a small pollinator hotel using simple materials and see who moves in.

Leave unplanted pockets for ground-nesting bees to burrow and butterflies to puddle.

Insects in the Garden

Meadow gardens are an invitation to wildlife to join you in your landscape. Greet them with curiosity. Many people grew up with a fear of insects due to limited understanding—myself included. Having a garden for wildlife offers you an opportunity to correct and overcome that misunderstanding. Think of your garden as a learning landscape. Welcome and identify the diversity of visitors.

Before you reach for a spray or seek out an all-natural pest control, wait. Keep a journal or list of the various insects that you see. Take notes on what species of plants attract which insects. Learn about the beneficial insects in your area and see if you can spot any in your meadow. Remember that insects go through various life stages so try to familiarize yourself with them so you know what you're observing. That caterpillar munching on your leaves could turn into a favorite butterfly.

Commit to being okay with some holes in your leaves. Step back and notice how most insect damage rarely takes away from the overall beauty of your garden. Set a loose threshold in your mind of how much damage you are willing to tolerate. Avoid pesticides, even organic or home-made, except in extreme cases. As I've gained more experience, I've found a direct relationship with my increased tolerance for insect damage. I take a much more "survival of the fittest" hands-off approach these days.

While I might squish some aphids on a young milkweed plant, I generally let the plants and insects work it out themselves. Often, I will see ladybug eggs and larvae already nearby. If I had reached for the insecticidal soap, I would have risked hurting these beneficials as well. This is an opportunity to watch and learn—with fascination. Over time with the correct maintenance practices, beneficial bugs will build up their population in your landscape and help keep the ecosystem there in balance.

A planting freshly cut back by hand in early spring.

When to Cut Back + Clean Up the Garden

When doing any landscape maintenance, always approach the task with the question, who are you managing the garden for? In the past, most garden maintenance prioritized tasks directed towards humans. The aesthetics of the garden was considered through the lens of what was fashionable for people. Other players in the past may have been livestock. For example, you may have mown your fields during the summer to harvest hay. Now that we're considering design and maintenance from a more ecological perspective, you have to ask yourself, beyond myself and my friends, who else am I managing my landscape for?

There will always be a trade-off of some kind when it comes to when to cut back and cleanup of your garden. Traditionally, gardens were tidied up in autumn. This made the landscape appear more cared for and deliberate. Refer to your goals to see what wildlife you wish to consider in your management and learn about their life cycles and how to support them. For example, if you'd like to attract ground-nesting solitary bee species, leave bare ground available and do not mulch. How and when you work in the garden will impact various species differently. Be clear about who else you are managing for and make your practices most attractive to them.

There's also a misconception that removing plant material and leaf litter reduces overwintering pests and diseases. We now know that these interactions are much more dynamic and complex than mere tidiness. If you have a problem with rust or another fungus on a certain species, remove the damaged foliage. Unless your home compost pile reaches 140°F (60°C) to kill pathogens, add it to your municipal compost bin. This is especially true in food and vegetable gardens. Aside from extreme infestations, an autumn cleanup does not reduce the possibility of pests or diseases that are ubiquitous and found throughout your landscape. Removing the plant material in fall reduces places for beneficial insects and other wildlife to overwinter.

Winter Interest

Winter interest is an important design consideration in climates with four seasons. The textures of architectural plants and the silhouettes of seed heads are particularly striking dusted in snow. If you have never considered winter interest before, search online or at the library for images and examples.

There are so many colors of brown that you will come to appreciate. While it is a more subdued palette, there is a great variety of color that will slowly bleach over the winter. I may cut back some of the plants that turn to mush after a hard frost, but I leave the majority untouched until early spring.

Clearing the Way for Spring Bulbs

If you create an extensive bulb layer that emerges early, I recommend cutting back your garden in late winter when the ground is frozen. Working when the ground is still frozen prevents compaction. Removing the previous year's plant material clears the way for the bulb display and prevents trampling later in the season. If you have the space, create a pile of this material off to the side and wait to shred or compost it until mid-spring.

ABOVE The tawny leaves and seedheads of liatris and milkweed look sculptural in the winter light.

OPPOSITE The subtle shift from early November (BOTTOM) to late December (TOP) as the bright colors slowly fade to shades of pink and brown.

Indian and switch grass stand tall in late autumn, providing cover for birds collecting seeds.

Overwintering Wildlife

While the aesthetic reason to leave plants standing for the off season is human focused, there are several benefits to the garden ecology. You've probably heard the slogan *leave the leaves*. This was created to encourage homeowners to reduce the amount of garden cleanup in favor of preserving habitat for wildlife.

There may be moth or butterfly caterpillars in the leaf litter or solitary bee larvae overwintering in the hollow stems of the perennials. While we have all heard of monarchs flying south during the cold months, most butterflies and moths do not migrate. They overwinter in some stage such as an egg, caterpillar, or chrysalis. Cleaning up the garden and removing the leaf litter also removes all of this tiny wildlife that you would otherwise support.

Leave the leaves typically means until spring. In some applications you may decide to only remove the leaf litter every few years, or to cut back only a portion of your garden—alternating each year. In the case of mini meadows where the groundcover layer has been designed and planted, it is best to remove most organic matter by spring. You can still leave the leaves somewhere on your property such as a woodland edge or behind the garden shed. Wait to compost them until late spring and don't pile them too deeply.

Certainly, the birds will appreciate seed heads of the dried flowers as a food source during the cold months. It doesn't make sense to cut back and compost your garden in the fall, only to go out and buy bagged bird food for your feeders. Queen bumblebees may overwinter in the dead vegetation or in a burrow just below the soil. Eggs of beneficial insects that keep the pests in check are also to be found in the various layers of dormant plants. If you remove this ecosystem in autumn, you are denying yourself the biodiversity you seek to attract.

Tools for Cutting Back

In late winter or early spring, begin cutting back your meadow. Depending on the size of your garden, this can be done in multiple ways. I prefer to use hand pruners because it gets me in close contact with all of the plants and allows for the most precision and close observation. It also lets me neatly collect the plant material as I go. However, this can be time consuming.

A hand sickle or scythe are other hand tool options that will slightly speed up the process. If you have a larger area or you'd like to get the job done faster, consider machinery such as a string trimmer or lawn mower. The advantage to these machines is they are quicker and reduce effort. The trade-off is that they are typically gas powered, noisy, and have a large carbon footprint. Battery-powered versions are "greener" choices overall, especially if you have solar panels or utilize green energy sources such as wind.

Cut everything back to four inches (10 cm). Using a leaf rake or leaf blower, remove the debris to a holding area before composting it later in the spring—either on site or through your municipality. If you don't have the space to keep it on site, wait until as late as possible to cut back to give overwintering wildlife the best chance of survival.

Snow collects on the seedheads of *Echinacea* and slowly collapses the slender grasses in late winter.

Cutting back with hand pruners allows for precision and close observation.

A scythe can be used to speed up the process without the use of power tools.

Another option to trial, depending on your soil conditions, is to chop the remaining plant material and leave it on site. Using a mulching mower set to the tallest cut height, pass though the space two to three times to shred and spread the remaining plant material. If you are having issues with an abundance of undesirable plants, plan to remove this material and compost it off site.

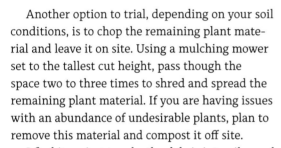

I find it easiest to rake the debris into piles and then onto a tarp. It should be quite light and easy to lift. Removing the debris helps to keep your soil lean, which is preferable for most meadow and prairie plants. The compost can later be used in your veggie garden, more traditional shrub and flower borders, or around the trees in your landscape. If you are working solo, be sure to not overfill your tarp so you can maneuver it easily. The biggest challenge is usually wind—so check the forecast before scheduling.

Saving Seeds

If you are interested in saving seeds, add a column in your plant list so you can add notes that are specific to the species you have selected. You will be finding tips on the best time and techniques to harvest and store the seed. You'll also find information on successful seed starting and germination practices, which you can add to another column.

Often, I direct scatter the seed in the garden and see what happens or leave the seed heads up for the winter and let the birds do the dispersing. If there are certain species that I am particularly interested in propagating, I will do my research and set a reminder in my calendar to scout for seeds. The opposite is also true. If there are certain species that I would like to limit the spread of, I also set a reminder and remove their spent flowers before they go to seed. You can save seed for future use on your property or to share with friends and neighbors.

Dynamic Meadows

Maintenance is as much a part of the design process as the initial site analysis or base plan. As you become more familiar with the species you have selected and how they interact in your garden, you will start to understand how to manage them. Meadow gardens are intentionally dynamic. I encourage you to let the plants you have selected begin to tell their story before you overly groom. Welcome the tight knit interactions by allowing a diversity of newcomers and keeping an eye on overly enthusiastic volunteers. These species interactions are a dance that is specific to your site and design intention—only you can decide who to edit or encourage.

Sharing Seeds and Divisions with Friends

As your garden begins to fill in, some of your plants will become large enough to divide—usually in year three or four. This is an opportunity to expand your meadow or share plants with others. Revisit your original design intention, paying careful attention to proportions, as well as plant health to determine which plants need to be split. While you can divide most plants throughout the growing season, you ideally want to do this in spring or fall when the days are cooler. Keep in mind that dividing while your plants are in bud or in flower may sacrifice the bloom for that year and unnecessarily stress the plant.

You may choose to research perennial maintenance by species and add these notes to your plant list or you may tackle all the divisions at the same time. Using a shovel, lift the entire plant. Be sure to collect an ample root ball. Depending on the size of the plant, use a sharp soil knife, shovel, or handsaw to half or quarter the rootzone. Return a section to the original location, top the hole off with unamended soil, and water generously. Pot up the extra divisions, water, and place them in a shaded area until they are ready for their new home. Remember, the best time to accomplish garden tasks is when you have the opportunity and energy to do so!

Once your garden has filled in, begin to monitor it for ripening seeds. On dry afternoons, collect those that are ready. I find paper lunch bags work well. Label the outside with a permanent marker. Depending on the quantity of seeds, collect and store individual species separately or create your own seed mixes. Leave the bags open in a cool dry covered location out of the sun to be sure they are free from moisture before storage. You may wish to further research related topics such as species-specific seed cleaning and germination requirements. Once dry, these seeds are now ready to share or exchange with others.

By sharing plants and seeds with others, you are encouraging them to create their own mini meadows. It gives you the opportunity to share your passion with your friends and neighbors—and a chance for you to learn from them. At the same time, you are keeping your own garden in balance aesthetically and your plants healthy. It's also fun to share any interesting wildlife associations you have learned about—stories to accompany the seeds and plant divisions.

Make notes of which species you'd like to collect seeds from.

Research cleaning and storage for each species you plan to include.

7

What to Plant

Plant Lists and Charts to Choose the Best Plants for Your Climate

Plant lists are an important way to organize your ideas. They can be as simple as a list of botanical names or include several columns with characteristics about each species. Over time I have begun using a similar format for most projects with as many categories as I see fit—varying by project objectives and intent. While spreadsheets may seem technical for a small garden, they allow for the information to be easily edited, sorted, and copied/pasted into new lists. For quick reference, I like to add a hyperlink for each species to connect to additional information or image searches. This chapter covers how to create a plant list for your mini meadow.

All in the Name

Start with the Latin names. This is the best way to ensure that you are referring to the correct plant species. Common names are fun, and appear easier to use and remember, but they tend to be regional and may lead to confusion. Often, several species will share the same, or similar, common names. I include them next to the botanical names. Botanical names are italicized and written as follows: *Genus species* 'Cultivar or Variety'. Common names are written in parenthesis in lowercase with only the proper nouns capitalized: (Virginia bluebell).

Additional Categories to Consider

To the left of the botanical names, create a column for quantities. If you are sourcing in flats, create a column for the number of plants per flat and one for the number of flats. Place all additional columns to the right of the common names.

Next, include columns for height and width. Use the average of the sizes you gathered in your research. This will make it easier to sort your list by height as a tool for organizing your layout and installation in advance. See pages 108–113 in the layout and installation strategies section regarding simplifying the heights and widths and grouping by ranges.

Include a column for type that includes categories such as: grass, perennial, annual, or bulb. I also include columns for bloom time and color. In the following lists I have used a range of seasons for bloom times such as early spring and late fall. These make it easier to approximate and sort when evaluating whether you have successfully achieved a meadow that is continuously blooming in your design.

I also include a column for layer. The terminology may change depending on the scale and complexity of your project, but in its simplest form, the layer column groups plants by height and intention. Categories such as emergent, mid-, low, and groundcover may suffice.

You may wish to further define your plants by adding a column identifying those with terms such as architectural, seasonal bloom, and/or matrix (intermixed). Architectural plants are those with strong silhouettes that persist over winter. Seasonal bloom reference less distinctive forms with strong visual impact in the weeks while they bloom. Matrix plants are those that intermix well and create visual harmony through their spontaneity and random repetition. Refer to page 71 in chapter three for more discussion on these terms.

Budget + Costs Categories

We have touched upon budget lightly elsewhere in this book. As mentioned in chapter three, I recommend brainstorming without a hard budget in mind. There are ways to achieve your desired outcomes without sacrificing your design or breaking the bank. When creating your plant list, include a column or two for costs. This will help you track your estimated and actually prices as

you begin to source the plant material. For those who have some familiarity with spreadsheets, there are simple ways to add formulas so that you can multiply the unit prices by the quantities of each species. This will allow you to play with the numbers as you begin fitting your dreamscape into your real budget.

You may wish to add a materials section below your plant list to track additional items you will need to acquire for your project. These may include tools, topsoil, mulch, propagation trays, seeds, site furnishings, and more. Create a list of everything you can think of and assign a realistic price to it based on research in your local area. You can then prioritize the items and phase their purchases as needed. Knowing the additional materials estimate will help keep you honest with your plant budget.

Create sub-totals and a total for plants and materials. Remember to include local taxes and any associated delivery fees. You may also wish to create a column for where you will source each of the items and species. If so, include a link to their website and/or their telephone number. Using a spreadsheet allows you to map out your approximate costs and tighten them with more accurate numbers as you continue your research. These practical items will keep you organized and your budget on track.

Leave Space for Notes

The notes column acts as a catch-all. This may include species-specific maintenance instructions, a space for observations, such as pest problems or pollinator associations, or any other tidbits you wish to include or record. Other possible columns may reference price per plant or flat, when the species will be available, installation time, and/or possible species substitutions. If you are propagating or collecting seed, include columns to record research and notes on these as well.

There is no one-size-fits-all approach. Include the information that you will use. Extra effort in creating your plant list will simplify your design and installation process, as well as the ongoing maintenance. A well organized and researched list will also be useful when creating future designs or when sharing information with friends and neighbors.

A General Reminder to Celebrate Native Plants

Keep in mind as you create your own plant lists and when referring to the lists on the following pages that part of the fun of a meadow garden is to invite your surroundings into your landscape. As some of your inspiration came from visiting wild spaces nearby, remember to celebrate your local aesthetic and unique sense of place. Native plants are adapted to local growing conditions and support your local wildlife. Prioritize species that you love coming across in natural areas nearby.

Sample Plant Lists

The lists on the following pages include species from around the globe. What may be native or well-behaved in one region may be aggressive or even invasive in another. It is critical to learn about the plants that have been determined to displace native plants in your area and make a commitment to avoid them. Cross-check to be sure none of the suggested plants you wish to use have been identified as invasive (or potentially invasive) where you live.

In some cases, when I have worked with multiple desirable species of the same plant, I have listed only the genus. Use this as an opportunity to see if there are locally native species in that

Pale blue camas or quamash (*Camassia leichtlinii* `Blue Heaven') silhouetted in front of apricot *Geums*

genus available for you to include in your design. Have fun and do your best to do no harm.

These lists are intended as a jumping off point to inspire you. I have included species that I have used in places where I have lived and worked. There are thousands of additional options and countless combinations. Find the intersection where beauty and function meet by researching what is right for your site, aesthetic, and local ecosystem.

Missouri goldenrod (*Solidago missouriensis*) and sea holly (*Eryngium planum*)

Dotted blazing star (*Liatris punctata*)

Mid-Height Dry Sun Plants

The plants in the following chart are good choices for moderate to dry sun locations in average to lean soils. They are mid-height flowering perennials varying from roughly eighteen to thirty inches (46–76 cm). The palette mixes well together in shades of blue, purple, orange, yellow, and white. Combine them with taller structural plants and lower spreading plants and groundcovers.

botanical name	common name	height	width	bloom time	color	native range
Agastache rupestris	sunset hyssop	24 in (60 cm)	30 in (76 cm)	mid-summer to early fall	orange-lavender	southwestern United States
Anaphalis margaritacea	pearly everlasting	24 in (60 cm)	18 in (46 cm)	late summer	white with yellow	Asia; North America
Artemisia frigida	fringed sage	12 in (30 cm)	12 in (30 cm)	late summer	yellow	Asia; eastern Europe; North America
Asclepias tuberosa	butterfly milkweed	18 in (46 cm)	12 in (30 cm)	mid- to late summer	orange-yellow	eastern and southern United States
Castilleja integra	wholeleaf Indian paintbrush	16 in (41 cm)	12 in (30 cm)	early summer to mid-fall	orange-red	southwestern United States

(continued)

OPPOSITE, TOP Sunset hyssop (*Agastache rupestris*) + Tennessee coneflower (*Echinacea tennesseensis*)
BOTTOM Sea holly (*Eryngium planum*) + Purple coneflower (*Echinacea purpurea*)

Purple prairie clover (*Dalea purpurea*)

Mid-Height Dry Sun Plants, *continued*

botanical name	common name	height	width	bloom time	color	native range
Dalea purpurea	purple prairie clover	18 in (46 cm)	18 in (46 cm)	mid- to late summer	rose-purple	North America
Echinacea angustifolia	narrow-leaf coneflower	18 in (46 cm)	12 in (30 cm)	mid-summer	light pink to pale purple	central North America
Erigeron speciosus	Aspen fleabane	24 in (60 cm)	18 in (46 cm)	late summer	purple	western North America
Eryngium planum	sea holly	24 in (60 cm)	18 in (46 cm)	mid-summer to early fall	steel blue	central and southeastern Europe
Kniphofia 'Mango Popsicle'	'Mango Popsicle' red hot poker	24 in (60 cm)	18 in (46 cm)	late spring to early summer	orange	garden variety
Liatris punctata	dotted blazing star	24 in (60 cm)	12 in (30 cm)	mid-summer to early fall	purple	central and mid-west North America

CLOCKWISE Butterfly milkweed (*Asclepias tuberosa*); Rocky Mountain penstemon (*Penstemon strictus*); pearly everlasting (*Anaphalis margaritacea*)

botanical name	common name	height	width	bloom time	color	native range
Limonium platyphyllum	sea lavender	24 in (60 cm)	24 in (60 cm)	late summer	lavender blue	southeastern and central Europe
Linum lewisii	prairie flax	18 in (46 cm)	12 in (30 cm)	mid- to late summer	blue	mid-west and western North America
Monarda punctata	spotted beebalm	20 in (51 cm)	12 in (30 cm)	early to mid-summer	cream, pink, and lavender	central and eastern United States and Canada; California
Salvia nemorosa 'Caradonna'	'Caradonna' meadow sage	18 in (46 cm)	18 in (46 cm)	mid-summer to early fall	blue-violet	Europe; Asia
Symphyotrichum oblongifolium 'Dream of Beauty'	'Dream of Beauty' aromatic aster	16 in (41 cm)	24 in (60 cm)	early fall to late fall	lavender-pink	northeastern and central United States

Emergent/Tall Dry Sun Plants

The following plants are tall emergent flowering perennials thirty inches (76 cm) or taller and are best suited for moderate to dry sun locations in average to lean soils. The palette includes purples, pinks, blues, oranges, yellows, and whites blooming from late spring to mid-autumn. Think of these as the statues of your garden that emerge above the rest of the planting.

botanical name	common name	height	width	bloom time	color	native range
Echinacea pallida	pale purple coneflower	30 in (76 cm)	18 in (46 cm)	mid-summer	pale purple	eastern and central North America
Echinacea purpurea	eastern purple coneflower	36 in (91 cm)	18 in (46 cm)	mid- to late summer	purple-pink	eastern North America
Echinops ritro	globe thistle	48 in (122 cm)	18 in (46 cm)	late summer to early fall	blue	central and eastern Europe; Asia
Eryngium yuccifolium	rattlesnake master	54 in (137 cm)	30 in (76 cm)	early summer to fall	greenish-white	United States
Kniphofia spp.	red hot poker	30 in (76 cm)	18 in (46 cm)	late spring to early summer	red, orange, yellow	Africa
Papaver orientale 'Helen Elizabeth'	'Helen Elizabeth' oriental poppy	36 in (91 cm)	18 in (46 cm)	early summer	salmon	Caucasus, northern Turkey; northern Iran
Penstemon strictus	Rocky Mountain penstemon	30 in (76 cm)	24 in (60 cm)	spring to early summer	blue	western North America
Peucedanum verticillare	giant milk parsley	96 in (244 cm)	24 in (60 cm)	mid-summer to fall	yellow	southeastern Europe; Asia
Phlomis russeliana	Jerusalem sage	36 in (91 cm)	18 in (46 cm)	mid-summer to fall	pale yellow	southwestern Asia
Salvia azurea var. *grandiflora*	blue sage	48 in (122 cm)	36 in (91 cm)	late summer to fall	blue	central North America

CLOCKWISE Pale purple coneflower (*Echinacea pallida*); giant milk parsley (*Peucedanum verticillare*); rattlesnake master (*Eryngium yuccifolium*)

Mesic to Wet Sun Plants

This list includes plants suited for average to wet soils in full sun. While these species prefer ample moisture, most require adequate drainage. Know your site conditions and select species accordingly. If you are planting within a rain garden or other spaces that get periodically inundated with water, read up on which species tolerate periodic standing water and which are better suited for the upper edges of the banks. Plants in this palette range from whites, pinks, and reds to yellows, blues, and purples. See the groundcover list on page 158 for additional suggestions for the ground plane.

botanical name	common name	height	width	layer	bloom time	color	native range
Asclepias incarnata	swamp milkweed	42 in (107 cm)	30 in (76 cm)	emergent	late summer	white; pink; mauve	northeastern and southeastern United States
Carex spp.	sedges	var.	var.	mid; low; groundcover	var.	greens; browns	var.
Eupatorium perfoliatum	boneset	60 in (152 cm)	42 in (107 cm)	emergent	late summer to fall	white	eastern United States
Eutrochium spp.	Joe-Pye weed	60 in (152 cm)	24 in (60 cm)	emergent	late summer to fall	purple-pink	North America
Filipendula rubra	queen of the prairie	72 in (183 cm)	42 in (107 cm)	emergent	mid- to late summer	pale pink	eastern United States
Iris versicolor	northern blue flag iris	24 in (60 cm)	24 in (60 cm)	mid	spring to early summer	violet blue	northeastern North America
Juncus effusus	soft rush	36 in (91 cm)	36 in (91 cm)	emergent	early to late summer	yellowish-green	Eurasia; North America; Australia; New Zealand

New York ironweed (*Vernonia noveboracensis*)

Boneset (*Eupatorium perfoliatum*)

botanical name	common name	height	width	layer	bloom time	color	native range
Liatris spicata	blazing star	36 in (91 cm)	12 in (30 cm)	low	late summer	red-purple	eastern United States
Lilium canadense	Canada lily	48 in (122 cm)	18 in (46 cm)	emergent	mid- to late summer	yellow to red	eastern North America
Lobelia cardinalis	cardinal flower	36 in (91 cm)	18 in (46 cm)	emergent	late summer to fall	scarlet red; white; rose	Americas
Lobelia siphilitica	great blue lobelia	30 in (76 cm)	14 in (36 cm)	mid	late summer to fall	blue	eastern North America
Sisyrinchium angustifolium	blue-eyed grass	20 in (51 cm)	9 in (23 cm)	groundcover	late spring to early summer	violet-blue	North America
Solidago rugosa	rough goldenrod	48 in (122 cm)	24 in (60 cm)	emergent	late summer to fall	yellow	eastern North America
Symphyotrichum novae-angliae	New England aster	40 in (122 cm)	30 in (76 cm)	emergent	late summer to fall	deep pink-purple	eastern North America
Verbena hastata	blue vervain	48 in (122 cm)	24 in (60 cm)	emergent	late summer to fall	purplish-blue	eastern North America
Vernonia noveboracensis	New York ironweed	60 in (152 cm)	42 in (107 cm)	emergent	late summer to fall	purple	eastern United States
Zizia aurea	golden Alexander	26 in (66 cm)	20 in (51 cm)	mid	mid-spring to early summer	yellow	eastern Canada to southern United States

Swamp milkweed (*Asclepias incarnata*)

Great blue lobelia (*Lobelia siphilitica*)

Blue vervain (*Verbena hastata*)

Grasses

Grasses are a quintessential component to any meadow garden. Here is a short list of my favorites. Include a mix of cool- and warm-season grasses to be sure to have interest throughout the growing months. Are there any grasses in your area that catch your eye? Consider selecting local native grasses to your garden to fill this design component.

botanical name	common name	height	width	layer	bloom time	color	native range
Bouteloua gracilis	blue grama	18 in (46 cm)	12 in (30 cm)	mid to low	mid- to late summer	tan	southern and western United States; Mexico
Carex spp.	sedges	var.	var.	mid; low; groundcover	var.	green to brown	var.
Carex buchananii 'Red Rooster'	'Red Rooster' leatherleaf sedge	18 in (46 cm)	18 in (46 cm)	mid to low	mid- to late summer	light brown	New Zealand
Deschampsia spp.	tufted hair grass	var.	var.	mid	var.	green to brown	var.
Erogrostis spectabilis	purple lovegrass	18 in (46 cm)	18 in (46 cm)	mid	late summer	soft reddish-purple	North America
Hakonechloa macra	Japanese forest grass	16 in (41 cm)	18 in (46 cm)	mid to low	late summer	yellow-green	Japan
Juncus effusus	soft rush	24 in (60 cm)	24 in (60 cm)	mid	late summer	yellowish-green	Eurasia; North America; Australia; New Zealand
Koeleria macrantha	prairie junegrass	18 in (46 cm)	12 in (30 cm)	mid to low	late spring to early summer	light green	Europe; Asia; North America
Panicum virgatum	switch grass	48 in (122 cm)	18 in (46 cm)	emergent	late summer to fall	wheat	North America
Schizachyrium scoparium	little bluestem	36 in (91 cm)	18 in (46 cm)	emergent	late summer to fall	wheat	eastern North America
Sorghastrum nutans	Indian grass	48 in (122 cm)	18 in (46 cm)	emergent	late summer to fall	copper	eastern and central United States
Sporobolus heterolepis	prairie dropseed	30 in (76 cm)	24 in (60 cm)	mid	late summer to fall	pink and brown	North America

CLOCKWISE Little bluestem (*Schizachyrium scoparium*); blue grama (*Bouteloua gracilis*), prairie junegrass (*Koeleria macrantha*), prairie dropseed (*Sporobolus heterolepis*), and more; Switch grass (*Panicum virgatum* 'Shenandoah')

Annuals

Annuals can be used on their own or as first-year color in a newly establishing perennial meadow. This list includes some of my favorites ranging in size from six inches to forty-two inches (15–107 cm) in a multitude of colors. I have deliberately not included recommended cultivars as there are too many to list. Check with your local nurseries to see what is available nearby and which will do best in your area. Refer to pages 66–67 for simple tips on how to work with color and create harmonious designs. Keep in mind the seed collection and self-seeding potential for many of these species. In some cases, you may welcome the volunteers and in other cases you may wish to remove the flower heads before they set seed to avoid unwanted seedlings. Note that depending on your growing climate, some annuals may perform as tender perennials and vice versa.

Lemon beebalm (*Monarda citriodora*)

botanical name	common name	height	width	layer	bloom time	color	native range
Agastache Arizona series	dwarf hummingbird mint	10 in (25 cm)	10 in (25 cm)	low to groundcover	early summer to late summer	orange; yellow; pink	garden origin
Ageratum houstonianum	floss flower	24 in (60 cm)	18 in (46 cm)	mid	summer through frost	blue; violet; red: white	Mexico
Celosia spicata	wheat celosia	36 in (91 cm)	24 in (60 cm)	emergent	summer to frost	purple; pink; rose	Africa; South America
Cleome spp.	spider flower	42 in (106 cm)	24 in (60 cm)	emergent	summer	white; pink; lavender; rose	South America
Cosmos bipinnatus	cosmos	36 in (91 cm)	30 in (76 cm)	emergent	early summer to frost	pink; red; white	Mexico; southern United States
Emilia javanica 'Irish Poet'	tassel flower	24 in (60 cm)	12 in (30 cm)	mid	mid-summer to fall	orange to red	tropical and sub-tropical Asia

(continued)

CLOCKWISE Globe amaranth (*Gomphrena* spp.) and snow-on-the-mountain (*Euphorbia marginata*); tassel flower (*Emilia javanica* 'Irish Poet'); Iceland poppy (*Papaver nudicaule* 'Champagne Bubbles Pink')

Annuals, *continued*

botanical name	common name	height	width	layer	bloom time	color	native range
Eschscholzia californica	California poppy	14 in (36 cm)	14 in (36 cm)	low to groundcover	mid-summer to fall	orange to orange-yellow	western United States
Euphorbia marginata	snow on the mountain	24 in (60 cm)	18 in (46 cm)	mid	summer to fall	white	temperate North America
Gomphrena spp.	globe amaranth	var.	var.	var.	early summer to frost	magenta; pink; purple; white; red; orange	central America; northeastern Mexico; New Mexico and Texas, USA
Monarda citriodora	lemon beebalm	24 in (60 cm)	12 in (30 cm)	mid	spring to late summer	lavender to pink to white	central and southern United States; northern Mexico
Nicotiana alata	flowering tobacco	48 in (122 cm)	18 in (46 cm)	emergent	summer to fall	yellow-green; white; pink; red; yellow	southern Brazil; northern Argentina; Paraguay; Colombia
Papaver rhoeas	corn poppy	14 in (36 cm)	9 in (23 cm)	low to groundcover	mid- to late summer	red (sometimes purple or white)	northern Africa; temperate Europe; Asia
Papaver somniferum	breadseed poppy	30 in (76 cm)	8 in (20 cm)	emergent	spring	blue; purple; pink; red; burgundy; white	southern Europe; northern Africa
Papaver nudicaule	Iceland poppy	14 in (36 cm)	6 in (15 cm)	low	spring to early summer	orange; salmon; yellow; rose; cream; white	subarctic Asia and North America; central Asia; temperate China
Viola tricolor	Johnny jump up	6 in (15 cm)	6 in (15 cm)	low to groundcover	early spring to late fall	purple; blue; yellow; white	Europe; Asia
Verbena bonariensis	tall verbena	36 in (91 cm)	24 in (60 cm)	emergent	summer to frost	rose-violet; lavender	South America
Zinnia elegans	common zinnia	36 in (91 cm)	12 in (30 cm)	emergent	summer to frost	pink; red; orange; yellow; green; lavender; white	Mexico

CLOCKWISE Cosmos (*Cosmos bipinnatus*) and 'Opopeo' amaranth (*Amaranthus* 'Opopeo'); common zinnia (*Zinnia elegans*); flowering tobacco (*Nicotiana alata*); tall verbena (*Verbena bonariensis*) and Mexican feathergrass (*Nassella tenuissima*)

Edible Plants

So many plants are edible and/or have medicinal properties. Proper identification is essential, as well as parts, preparation, and quantities. Find trusted sources for information. Ideally, learn from an expert. Beware of lookalikes and only consume plants if you are certain of what you are eating. *When in doubt, don't.*

Here is a list of edible plant species that lend themselves to a meadow-style garden. Refer to the "edible parts" column to see which parts are edible. Be sure the plants you purchase are labeled correctly and get more information on each before consuming. Select organically grown plant stock and ask the nursery about any recent chemical applications or grow from seed yourself.

Common yarrow (*Achillea millefolium*)

botanical name	common name	height	width	type
Achillea millefolium	common yarrow	24 in (60 cm)	24 in (60 cm)	perennial
Agastache foeniculum	anise hyssop	36 in (91 cm)	24 in (60 cm)	perennial
Allium schoenoprasum	chives	14 in (36 cm)	14 in (36 cm)	bulb
Borago officinalis	borage	24 in (60 cm)	14 in (36 cm)	annual
Echinacea purpurea	purple coneflower	36 in (91 cm)	18 in (46 cm)	perennial
Foeniculum vulgare	fennel	60 in (152 cm)	24 in (60 cm)	perennial
Matricaria chamomilla (syn. *recutita*)	German chamomile	18 in (46 cm)	10 in (25 cm)	annual
Matteuccia struthiopteris	ostrich fern	60 in (152 cm)	42 in (107 cm)	perennial
Monarda didyma	wild beebalm	36 in (91 cm)	30 in (76 cm)	perennial
Salvia elegans	pineapple sage	42 in (107 cm)	30 in (76 cm)	tender perennial
Symphyotrichum novae-angliae	New England aster	48 in (122 cm)	30 in (76 cm)	perennial
Tropaeolum majus	common nasturtium	12 in (30 cm)	24 in (60 cm)	annual
Verbascum thapsus	common mullein	54 in (137 cm)	24 in (60 cm)	biennial
Verbena hastata	blue vervain	48 in (122 cm)	24 in (60 cm)	perennial
Viola spp.	violets (certain species)	var.	var.	perennial

Common nasturtium (*Tropaeolum majus*)

Pineapple sage (*Salvia elegans*)

Blue vervain (*Verbena hastata*)

Purple coneflower (*Echinacea purpurea*)

layer	bloom time	color	edible parts	native range
mid	early summer to fall	white	leaves	Europe; western Asia; North America
emergent	early summer to fall	lavender to purple	leaves; flowers	northern North America
low	early to mid-spring	purple	leaves; young flowers	temperate Northern Hemisphere
mid	early to late summer	blue	young leaves; flowers	Europe
emergent	early to late summer	purple; pink; yellow; orange; white	leaves; petals	central and eastern North America
emergent	mid-summer	yellow	leaves; seeds	Mediterranean
low	early to late summer	white with yellow center	flowers	Europe; western Asia
emergent	none	n/a	furled up fiddlehead	Europe; eastern Asia; eastern North America
emergent	late summer	red; purple; pink	leaves; flowers	Canada; United States
emergent	late summer to mid-fall	red; purple; pink	leaves; flowers	Mexico; Guatemala
emergent	late summer to fall	deep pink-purple	leaves; flowers	eastern North America
low	mid-spring to fall	red; orange; yellow; salmon; purple	leaves; buds; flowers; buds; pods; seeds	Central and South America
emergent	early summer to fall	yellow	flowers; leaves	Europe; Asia
emergent	mid-summer to fall	purplish-blue	leaves; flowers (raw); seeds (roasted)	eastern North America
low to groundcover	varies	purple; white	leaves; stems; flowers	(most) temperate Northern Hemisphere

BOTH Meadowrue (*Thalictrum* spp.)   Hellebore (*Helleborus* sp.)   Virginia bluebells
(*Mertensia virginica*)

Part-Shade Plants

As we learned in chapter two, meadows are not just for full sun locations. While most plants bloom best with some sun, there are many flowering species that will perform well in part shade. Remember, part shade means four to six hours of sunlight per day, but not necessarily during the middle of the day. Here is a list of part-shade plant species from groundcovers to tall emergent plants blooming from early spring to fall.

botanical name	common name	height	width	layer	bloom time	color	native range
Anemonastrum canadense (syn. *Anemone canadensis*)	Canada anemone	18 in (46 cm)	24 in (60 cm)	low	spring to early summer	white	North America
Aquilegia spp.	columbine	var.	var.	mid	mid-spring to mid-summer	varies	Northern Hemisphere
Aruncus dioicus	goat's beard	60 in (152 cm)	36 in (91 cm)	emergent	early to mid-spring	cream	temperate Northern Hemisphere
Astilbe spp.	astilbe	var.	var.	mid	var.	white; pink; red; lavender	Asia; North America
Carex spp.	sedges	var.	var.	mid; low; groundcover	var.	green; tan; brown; pink	global
Digitalis spp.	foxgloves	var.	var.	emergent to mid	late spring to late summer	purple; pink; white; yellow	Europe; western Asia; northwestern Africa
Epimedium spp.	epimedium	10 in (25 cm)	24 in (60 cm)	low to groundcover	spring	red; orange; yellow; pink; purple; white	Asia; Mediterranean
Eurybia divaricata	white wood aster	24 in (60 cm)	24 in (60 cm)	mid	late summer to fall	white with yellow to red centers	eastern North America
Filipendula rubra	queen-of-the-prairie	72 in (183 cm)	42 in (107 cm)	emergent	mid-summer to fall	pale pink	eastern United States

Canada anemone
(*Anemonastrum canadense*)

Columbine (*Aquilegia* sp.)

Woodland phlox (*Phlox divaricata*)

botanical name	common name	height	width	layer	bloom time	color	native range
Geranium maculatum	wild geranium	18 in (46 cm)	18 in (46 cm)	low to groundcover	early to mid-spring	pale pink; deep pink; lilac	eastern United States
Hakonechloa macra	Japanese forest grass	16 in (41 cm)	18 in (46 cm)	mid to low	late summer to fall	yellow-green	Japan
Helleborus spp.	hellebores	18 in (46 cm)	18 in (46 cm)	low to groundcover	late winter to early spring	purple; pink; cream; yellow; green; black	Europe; Asia
Heuchera spp.	coral bells	var.	var.	low to groundcover	spring	white; green; pink; red	North America
Iris cristata	dwarf crested iris	8 in (20 cm)	9 in (23 cm)	groundcover	spring	pale blue	northeastern United States
Juncus effusus	soft rush	24 in (60 cm)	24 in (60 cm)	emergent	mid-summer	yellowish-green	Eurasia; North America; Australia; New Zealand
Mertensia virginica	Virginia bluebells	18 in (46 cm)	14 in (36 cm)	low to groundcover	early to mid-spring	blue	North America
Phlox divaricata	woodland phlox	9 in (23 cm)	9 in (23 cm)	low to groundcover	spring	rose-lavender; violet-blue	eastern North America
Symphyotrichum cordifolium	blue wood aster	36 in (91 cm)	18 in (46 cm)	mid	late summer to fall	blue with yellow centers	eastern and central North America
Thalictrum spp.	meadowrue	var.	var.	var.	var.	white; pink; cream; purple	temperate Northern Hemisphere; south to South Africa and tropical South America
Tricyrtis spp.	toad lily	20 in (51 cm)	18 in (46 cm)	mid	summer to fall	white; yellow; purple; pink (often spotted)	Asia; North America
Veronicastrum virginicum	Culver's root	60 in (152 cm)	36 in (91 cm)	emergent	early summer to fall	white; pink; pale blue	northeastern North America

Groundcovers

Groundcovers, also called green or living mulch, are an under-appreciated but valuable layer in your garden. As covered in chapter three, they provide many benefits, including weed suppression and moisture retention. Here is a list of possibilities from full sun to shade. Remember, even if you have a full-sun site, the groundcover may be partially shaded by the taller species in your design, so select accordingly.

The groundcover species listed with taller heights have mostly low basal foliage throughout the year and get their height from their flower stalks, which is why they're included here. When selecting groundcovers, look for plants that will spread non-aggressively to avoid outcompeting their neighbors. Choose species appropriate for the moisture levels and other conditions of your site.

botanical name	common name	height	width	sun/ shade	bloom time	color	native range
PART-SHADE TOLERANT							
Ajuga reptans	bugleweed	6 in (15 cm)	9 in (23 cm)	full sun to part shade	late spring to early summer	blue	Europe; northern Africa; southwestern Asia
Asarum canadense	wild ginger	9 in (23 cm)	14 in (36 cm)	part shade to full shade	spring	purplish-brown	eastern Canada and United States
Carex spp.	sedges	var.	var.	var.	var.	green; tan; brown; pink	global
Chrysogonum virginianum	green and gold	9 in (23 cm)	12 in (30 cm)	part shade to full shade	mid-spring to fall	yellow	eastern United States
Eurybia macrophylla	large-leaved aster	36 in (91cm)	36 in (91cm)	part shade to full shade	fall	violet or blue with yellow centers	eastern and central North America
Galium odoratum	sweet woodruff	9 in (23 cm)	12 in (30 cm)	part shade to full shade	early to mid-spring	white	northern Africa; Asia; Europe
Sedum ternatum	woodland stonecrop	4 in (10 cm)	8 in (20 cm)	full sun to part shade	early to mid-spring	white	eastern United States
Tiarella cordifolia	foamflower	9 in (23 cm)	18 in (46 cm)	part shade to full shade	spring	white; pink	eastern Canada and United States
Viola spp.	violets	var.	var.	var.	var.	purple; white	(most) temperate Northern Hemisphere
Waldsteinia fragarioides	barren strawberry	4 in (10 cm)	9 in (23 cm)	full sun to part shade	mid-spring	yellow	eastern United States

Foamflower (*Tiarella cordifolia*)

Small-leaf pussytoes (*Antennaria parvifolia*)

botanical name	common name	height	width	sun/shade	bloom time	color	native range
				SUN-TOLERANT			
Allium cernuum	nodding onion	14 in (36 cm)	4 in (10 cm)	full sun to part shade	mid- to late spring	pink	Canada to Mexico
Antennaria parvifolia	small-leaf pussytoes	4 in (10 cm)	8 in (20 cm)	full sun to part shade	late summer to early fall	grayish white	western Canada and United States
Antennaria rosea	rosy pussytoes	8 in (20 cm)	10 in (25 cm)	full sun to part shade	mid- to late summer	red-pink; yellow; white	central and western Canada and United States; Baja California, Mexico
Betonica (syn. *Stachys*) *officinalis*	betony	18 in (46 cm)	14 in (36 cm)	low to groundcover	late spring to summer	reddish-purple; pink	northern Africa; western Asia; Europe
Campanula rotundifolia	harebell	12 in (30 cm)	9 in (23 cm)	full sun to part shade	early summer to fall	blue	temperate Northern Hemisphere
Erigeron compositus	cutleaf daisy	6 in (15 cm)	8 in (20 cm)	full sun to part shade	late spring to mid-summer	white, pink; blue	eastern Russia; western Canada and United States
Eriogonum umbellatum	sulphur-flower buckwheat	10 in (25 cm)	24 in (60 cm)	full sun to part shade	late spring to mid-summer	yellow; cream	southwestern North America
Geum triflorum	prairie smoke	12 in (30 cm)	8 in (20 cm)	full sun to part shade	late spring to mid-summer	reddish-pink; purple	northern North America
Penstemon procerus	littleflower penstemon	12 in (30 cm)	8 in (20 cm)	full sun to part shade	early to late summer	blue-purple	western North America
Penstemon virens	blue mist penstemon	8 in (20 cm)	12 in (30 cm)	full sun to part shade	late spring to early summer	blue-purple	western United States

(continued)

Nodding onion (*Allium cernuum*)

Moss phlox (*Phlox subulata*)

Groundcovers, *continued*

botanical name	common name	height	width	sun/ shade	bloom time	color	native range
SUN-TOLERANT							
Phlox subulata	moss phlox	4 in (10 cm)	18 in (46 cm)	full sun to part shade	early to mid-spring	red-purple; violet purple; pink; white	eastern and central United States
Pulsatilla patens	eastern pasqueflower	8 in (20 cm)	4 in (10 cm)	full sun to part shade	early to mid-spring	blue-violet	western and northern North America; northern Europe; Siberia
Sedum spp.	sedum; stonecrop	var.	var.	full sun to part shade	var.	pink; red; purple; yellow	Northern Hemisphere extending into Africa and South America
Sphaeralcea coccinea	scarlet globemallow	10 in (25 cm)	10 in (25 cm)	full sun to part shade	mid-spring to late fall	orange-pink	mid-west and western North America
Symphyotrichum oblongifolium	aromatic aster	24 in (60 cm)	24 in (60 cm)	full sun to part shade	late summer to fall	blue; purple	northeastern and central United States

Eastern pasqueflower (*Pulsatilla patens*)

Harebell (*Campanula rotundifolia*)

Camas; quamash (*Camassia leichtlinii* 'Blue Heaven')

Ornamental onion (*Allium* spp.)

Bulbs + Bulb-Like Plants

Bulbs are a fantastic way to extend your bloom season into early spring as well as add drama in summer months. The following is a list of fall- and spring-planted bulbs. As traditional bulb displays can be static and formal, selection and placement are key to incorporating into a stylized meadow design.

Use a lot. For smaller species, plant handfuls together. Dig large holes to the depth required of the bulb species, scatter, turn upright where they land, and cover with soil. Position larger bulbs randomly—some close, some spread apart. When planting in groups, select different numbers to place together. Emulate the whimsical patterns in nature. Apply the design elements discussed starting on page 63 in chapter three and the layout and installation strategies on pages 108–111 in chapter five.

botanical name	common name	height	spacing	layer	bloom time	color	native range
FALL-PLANTED BULBS							
Allium christophii	star of Persia allium	18 in (46 cm)	12 in (30 cm)	mid	mid-spring	pale lavender	western Asia; southeastern Europe
Allium sphaerocephalon	drumstick allium	30 in (76 cm)	3 in (8 cm)	emergent	mid-spring to mid-summer	deep green to rose-purple	Europe; northern Africa; western Asia
Allium 'Gladiator'	'Gladiator' allium	42 in (104 cm)	10 in (25 cm)	emergent	late spring to early summer	reddish-purple	garden origin
Allium 'Globemaster'	'Globemaster' allium	24 in (60 cm)	12 in (30 cm)	mid	spring	deep lavender	garden origin
Allium 'Mount Everest'	'Mount Everest' allium	36 in (91 cm)	8 in (20 cm)	emergent	late spring to early summer	white	garden origin
Allium 'Purple Sensation'	'Purple Sensation' allium	24 in (60 cm)	8 in (20 cm)	mid	spring to early summer	purple	garden origin
Allium lusitanicum 'Summer Beauty'	'Summer Beauty' allium	18 in (46 cm)	18 in (46 cm)	mid	early summer to fall	pink	garden origin
Allium 'Summer Drummer'	'Summer Drummer' allium	54 in (137 cm)	12 in (30 cm)	emergent	late spring to early summer	pale purple and white	garden origin

(continued)

Foxtail lily (*Eremurus* spp.)

Pineapple lily (*Eucomis* sp.)

Dahlia (*Dahlia* sp.)

Bulbs + Bulb-Like Plants, *continued*

botanical name	common name	height	spacing	layer	bloom time	color	native range
FALL-PLANTED BULBS							
Camassia spp.	camas; quamash	var.	var.	var.	spring	blue; purple; lilac; white	North America
Colchicum speciosum	giant meadow saffron	12 in (30 cm)	10 in (25 cm)	low	mid-fall	reddish-violet	northern Turkey; Iran; Caucasus
Crocus speciosus	Bieberstein's crocus	4 in (10 cm)	4 in (10 cm)	low	early fall	lilac-blue	Turkey; Iran; Crimea
Crocus spp.	spring-blooming crocus	6 in (15 cm)	3 in (8 cm)	low	early spring to spring	purple, orange, yellow, pink, white	Mediterranean; North Africa; central and southern Europe; Middle East; central Asia; western China
Eremurus 'Moneymaker'	'Moneymaker' foxtail lily	60 in (152 cm)	24 in (60 cm)	emergent	mid- to late summer	lemon-yellow	garden origin
Eremurus 'Spring Valley Splendor'	'Spring Valley Splendor' foxtail lily	60 in (152 cm)	24 in (60 cm)	emergent	late spring to early summer	creamy peach-pink	garden origin
Eremurus x *isabellinus* 'Cleopatra'	'Cleopatra' foxtail lily	54 in (137 cm)	24 in (60 cm)	emergent	late spring to early summer	tangerine orange	garden origin

Spring-blooming crocus (*Crocus* spp.)

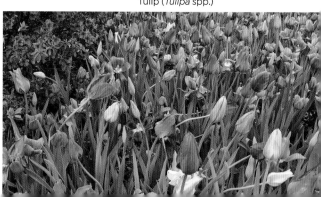

Tulip (*Tulipa* spp.)

Siberian squill (*Scilla sibirica*)

Dahlia (*Dahlia* sp.)

Foxtail lily (*Eremurus* sp.)

botanical name	common name	height	spacing	layer	bloom time	color	native range
FALL-PLANTED BULBS							
Fritillaria meleagris	snake's head fritillary	12 in (30 cm)	3 in (8 cm)	low	mid-spring	checkered reddish-brown, purple, white, and gray	western Asia; Europe
Galanthus nivalis	snowdrops	4 in (10 cm)	4 in (10 cm)	low	late winter to early spring	white and green	western Asia; eastern Europe
Gladiolus communis ssp. *byzantinus*	Byzantine gladiolus	24 in (60 cm)	6 in (15 cm)	mid	mid- to late spring	pink; purple-red	Spain; northwest Africa; Sicily
Lycoris squamigera	resurrection lily	20 in (51 cm)	6 in (15 cm)	mid	late summer to early fall	rose-pink w lilac	Japan
Muscari spp.	grape hyacinth	6 in (15 cm)	2 in (5 cm)	low	early spring to early summer	light blue; dark blue; lavender; white; pink	Mediterranean; northern Africa; central and southern Europe; western and central Asia
Narcissus spp.	daffodil	var.	var.	low	early spring to spring	white, yellow, apricot, peach; orange; cream	Europe; North Africa; garden origin

(continued)

'Summer Beauty' allium (*Allium lusitanicum* 'Summer Beauty')

Sicilian honey garlic (*Nectaroscordum siculum*)

Dahlia (*Dahlia* sp.)

Resurrection lily (*Lycoris squamigera*)

Bulbs + Bulb-Like Plants, *continued*

botanical name	common name	height	spacing	layer	bloom time	color	native range
FALL-PLANTED BULBS							
Nectaroscordum siculum	Sicilian honey garlic	42 in (197 cm)	18 in (46 cm)	emergent	late spring to early summer	cream, pink, and green	southern France and Italy
Scilla siberica	Siberian squill	6 in (15 cm)	6 in (15 cm)	low	early spring	blue; purple; lilac; white	Russia
Tulipa spp.	tulip	var.	var.	low	early, mid–, late spring	red; orange; yellow; pink; purple; white; cream; multi	southeastern Europe; Iberian peninsula; North Africa; Near East; Central Asia
SPRING-PLANTED BULBS							
Amaryllis belladonna	belladonna lily	30 in (76 cm)	9 in (23 cm)	emergent	summer	pink; red-burgundy	South Africa; Cape
Crocosmia spp.	crocosmia	30 in (76 cm)	6 in (15 cm)	emergent	summer	red; orange; yellow	southern and eastern Africa
Dahlia spp.	dahlia	var.	var.	var.	summer to fall	red; orange; yellow; pink; purple; white; cream	North America; Central America; garden origin
Eucomis spp.	pineapple lily	16 in (41 cm)	9 in (23 cm)	mid	summer	purple; pink; peach; green; white	southern Africa
Nerine bowdenii	Guernsey lily	16 in (41 cm)	4 in (10 cm)	mid	early to late fall	pink; red-burgundy	South Africa

Conclusion

You now have the tools to seek the inspiration and information necessary to design and install a mini meadow of your own. Inspired by the wild areas and designed spaces that bring you joy, you've created a new version of a garden—where beauty meets habitat and choices center around wildlife and ecosystem health as well as aesthetics. You learned how to identify your goals to inform your choices and carefully select plants that thrive together on your site.

By choosing a landscape filled with species local to your region, and managing it holistically and organically, you are supporting biodiversity in a far greater way than traditional lawns and ornamental perennial borders. Your gardens will be alive with pollinators and other wildlife all while reducing the amount of maintenance and inputs that more traditional landscapes require.

Gardening is about learning. Mistakes and lessons are part of the process. This book offers you a foundation on which to refer back to again and again. Take your time with each step and keep notes. Make informed choices, but allow yourself the freedom to experiment. Meadows are dynamic living systems. Give your creations time to reveal themselves to you. Set an intention with your research and choices and let nature add her dose of creativity. After all, that's the whimsy we meadow-makers seek.

Late August in Longwood Gardens' 86-acre (35 hectare) Meadow Garden in Kennett Square, Pennsylvania, USA.

Resources + Inspiration

RECOMMENDED READING

The Art of Gardening: Design Inspiration and Innovative Planting Techniques from Chanticleer
R. William Thomas

Attracting Native Pollinators: Protecting North America's Bees and Butterflies
The Xerces Society + Dr. Marla Spivak

Bringing Nature Home: How You Can Sustain Wildlife with Native Plants | Douglas W. Tallamy

Gardens of the High Line: Elevating the Nature of Modern Landscapes | Piet Oudolf + Rick Darke

Garden Revolution: How Our Landscapes Can Be a Source of Environmental Change
Larry Weaner + Thomas Christopher

The Know Maintenance Perennial Garden
Roy Diblik

Naturalistic Planting Design: The Essential Guide
Nigel Dunnett

A New Garden Ethic: Cultivating Defiant Compassion for an Uncertain Future
Benjamin Vogt

New Naturalism: Designing and Planting a Resilient, Ecologically Vibrant Home Garden | Kelly D. Norris

Plant-Driven Design: Creating Gardens That Honor Plants, Place, and Spirit
Scott Ogden + Lauren Springer Ogden

Planting: A New Perspective
Piet Oudolf + Noel Kingsbury

Planting in a Post-Wild World: Designing Plant Communities for Resilient Landscapes
Thomas Rainer + Claudia West

Sowing Beauty: Designing Flowering Meadows from Seed | James Hitchmough

RECOMMENDED GARDENS

THE HIGH LINE
New York, New York, USA

LURIE GARDEN
Chicago, Illinois, USA

DENVER BOTANIC GARDENS
Denver, Colorado, USA

CHANTICLEER: A PLEASURE GARDEN
Wayne, Pennsylvania, USA

COASTAL MAINE BOTANIC GARDENS
Boothbay, Maine, USA

LADY BIRD JOHNSON WILDFLOWER GARDEN
Austin, Texas, USA

NATIVE FLORA GARDEN @ BROOKLYN BOTANIC GARDEN
Brooklyn, New York, USA

THE MEADOW GARDEN @ LONGWOOD GARDENS
Kennett Square, Pennsylvania, USA

HERMANNSHOF
Weinheim, Germany

HUNTING BROOK GARDENS
Blessington Co., Wicklow, Ireland

GREAT DIXTER
East Sussex, England

BARBICAN ESTATE
London, England

QUEEN ELIZABETH OLYMPIC PARK
London, England

GREY TO GREEN
Sheffield, England

DESIGNERS + PLANT PEOPLE

ARJAN BOEKEL | Netherlands

TOM DE WITTE | Netherlands

PIET OUDOLF | Netherlands

ROY DIBLIK | USA

KELLY D. NORRIS | USA

THOMAS RAINER, PHYTO STUDIO | USA

LARRY WEANER | USA

CLAUDIA WEST, PHYTO STUDIO | USA

KEVIN PHILIP WILLIAMS | USA

ADAM WOODRUFF | USA

NIGEL DUNNETT | UK

JIMI BLAKE | UK

JAMES HITCHMOUGH | UK

NOEL KINGSBURY | UK

DAN PEARSON | UK

SARA PRICE | UK

TOM STUART-SMITH | UK

CASSIAN SCHMITT | Germany

BETTINA JAUGSTETTER | Germany

BEN O'BRIEN, WILD BY DESIGN | Canada

TOPICS + HASHTAGS

New Perennial Movement

Dutch Wave

New German Style

Naturalistic Garden

Naturalistic Planting

Matrix Planting

Perennial Meadows

Planting Design

Native Plants

Native Flora

+ the designers mentioned at left

PREVIOUS SPREAD Seedheads and autumn colors on a busy streetside planting designed by Denver Botanic Gardens horticulturist Kevin Philip Williams in Colorado, USA.

About the Author

Growing up on Narragansett Bay in Rhode Island, **Graham Laird Gardner** developed an early affinity for the diversity of the coastline and forests around him. A love for gardens and landscapes soon followed with summers spent working at farmer's markets, tending backyard gardens, and eventually designing outdoor spaces for his own clients.

After spending time at Vassar College and the Massachusetts College of Art and Design, Graham discovered Landscape Architecture at the University of Rhode Island, which helped him synthesize his artistic talents and passion for design, plants, and the spaces where they live. By this time, he had joined the Board of the Rhode Island Wild Plant Society, read Doug Tallamy's book, *Bringing Nature Home*, and realized the importance of a "sense of place" in design—for both ecological and aesthetic reasons.

Living in places as diverse as Rhode Island, Colorado, and Puerto Rico deepened Graham's appreciation for endemic landscapes and how different they are from one another. Graham uses his skills at reading the landscape and spending time observing to inform his design solutions and the way he approaches landscape enhancements and regeneration. It was later in life, living in a city without access to a yard, where he found his connection to growing food. Since then, he has pursued a better understanding for, and connection with, agroecology—and how food, wildlife, and beauty coexist and enhance one other.

Graham has over twenty-five years of experience in landscape design and project management in public, private, and non-profit sectors. Beyond his residential design projects, he has worked with agencies such as the Denver Parks Department, the United States Fish and Wildlife Service, the Rhode Island Natural History Survey, as well as many Cooperative Extension offices, friends of parks groups, and native plant societies.

Graham's diverse experiences, in New England, Colorado, California, and Puerto Rico, have instilled and reinforced his passion to influence and guide the public on best management practices and the importance of creating unique spaces inspired by nearby natural plant communities.

During his professional career, Graham has gained considerable practical experience in strategic and master planning, site analysis, regenerative landscape design, construction oversight, and landscape maintenance. As we move away from the thirsty lawns of the City Beautiful Movement designs of the early twentieth century toward a more ecological approach to green spaces, Graham is a leader in the new paradigm of high-functioning, water-smart, and low-maintenance landscapes.

Acknowledgments

So . . . I've written my first book. This would not have been possible without the direction and patience of my editor, Jessica Walliser, who first saw promise in me and gave me the opportunity and confidence to bring this book to life. A big thanks to the incredibly talented plantsman, designer, and author Kelly D. Norris, who first connected me to Jessica back when this book was just a seed.

I found the pause to write in large part because of the trust and generosity of two families who graciously welcomed me into their homes and found ways for me to contribute while giving me the time and space to create this book. To Ryan, Ashley, and Emmett, I will never forget the special times we got to share living at the reef and exploring the islands together. Thank you for your daily words of encouragement and all the support you continue to give.

To my current family, Daniella, Dani, Cyán, y Río—muchas gracias por todo. It has been a dream to land in the mountains in your beautiful home and learn from each of you. Daniella, thank you for effortlessly showing me how much there is to celebrate, how to deeply nourish body and soul, and for introducing me to so many beautiful people.

To Lynn for arriving right when I needed your guidance and healing energy. Thank you for teaching me about the laws of attraction and helping me reconnect with my higher self and inner voice.

To my parents Randy and Sandi, for your love, guidance, and late-night chats; for all the doors you opened because of your hard work and

The birdhouse (a bird blind for viewing birds) at the Pollinator Gardens at the Arboretum at Penn State University designed by Phyto Studio.

dedication to family; for believing in me and your lifelong support. To Nate, Emily, and Jackson, thank you for your love, encouragement, and laughter. Your support has been felt from afar.

To my Denver, Rhode Island, and Puerto Rico friends and colleagues—thank you for your ears, shoulders, arms, and wings—I have so many homes and so many I call family.

Thank you to the whole team at Quarto for your patience and expertise. This would not have been possible without each of your contributions. And to my fellow designers who contributed photography and inspiration—and allowed me to bounce ideas off of them: Adam, Benjamin, Claudia, Hayden, Kevin, and Scott—thank you!

And lastly, thank you to all the bad-ass plant-loving women who helped instill my passion for ecology, soil, and horticulture—who stretched my design (and people) skills—whether it was at a board meeting, volunteer event, garden tour, plant nursery, or wildflower hike! I'm thankful that I've attracted you into my life: Allie, Barclay, Beth, Catherine, Dani, Holly, Hope, Jane, Jenny, Julie, Karen, Kate, Kathleen, Nancy, Tysh, and Vanessa and SO MANY more.

I'm overwhelmed with gratitude and think of each of you with such fondness and admiration. To everyone I have encountered—you have each helped shape who I have become and what I value and give importance to—and, as such, you have each helped shape the contents, details, and imagery of this book.

Go plant a meadow or pause in one—zoom in on the tiny details that make life so exquisite. Tiny meadows provide for us all—plant lovers and pollinators alike—at a time when we are recognizing that what our landscapes do for the local ecology is more important than pure aesthetic goals. Tiny meadows are for everyone and everything—and we all benefit from their creation.

Thank you, thank you, thank you!
—graham

Index